# HOW TO RELAX
## A HOLISTIC APPROACH TO STRESS MANAGEMENT

**JOHN D. CURTIS**

University of Wisconsin, La Crosse

**RICHARD A. DETERT**

University of Wisconsin, La Crosse

 Mayfield Publishing Company

For Beata Jencks and John Kaestner—
friends, teachers, unique people from
whom we have learned much

Library of Congress Catalog Card Number: 80-84021
International Standard Book Number 0-87484-527-0

Manufactured in the United States of America
Mayfield Publishing Company
285 Hamilton Avenue, Palo Alto, California 94301

*Sponsoring editor:* C. Lansing Hays
*Managing editor:* Judith Ziajka
*Manuscript editor:* Carol Talpers
*Designer:* Nancy Sears
*Compositor:* HMS Typography
*Production manager:* Michelle Hogan
*Printer and binder:* George Banta Company

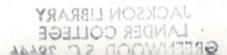

# CONTENTS

# PREFACE

As members of modern society, we face a multitude of changes in our personal and professional lives. During the 1970s, it became apparent that many aspects of our lives are governed by people and events beyond our control. Jobs, salaries, and the costs of food, gasoline, automobiles, and medical care have been jeopardized by inflation and by events taking place across the globe. This loss of control and increased vulnerability, in an environment of rapid growth, expanding technology, increased knowledge level, and changing sexual roles, requires adjustments. Lack of adequate time to adjust causes stress. As a result, stress management is becoming an important part of successful living in modern society.

Many people can adjust quickly to the rapidly changing conditions they face, but others do not adjust as well. This book provides a variety of stress management strategies that can be used by those who have difficulty adjusting and are experiencing stress as well as techniques and alternative strategies for those who adjust easily.

This book is based on a stress management program that was conceptualized by the principle author in 1972. The program has been further developed and refined by both authors since that time, as they worked with over two thousand clients in classes and individually. The program follows a step-by-step sequence and progresses from the basics to more advanced exercises. This book was designed to bridge the gap between knowledge and theory on one hand and practical application on the other. It was written as a practical and enjoyable workbook to give the reader an understanding of stress management. It includes suggested activities and practice schedules to help develop the individual stress management skills.

We would like to emphasize that, as health educators, we believe stress management is *not* a cure-all by itself, nor is it more important than other phases of health. To enhance and increase health, all facets of health—including fitness, nutrition, and mental/emotional health—must be looked at. Stress management is but one facet.

This book was designed and written for healthy people in an effort to provide information that will help them maintain and enhance their health. If you are under any type of medical supervision, the practice of the exercises presented in this book should take place under medical guidance. People with asthma, coronary heart disease, epilepsy, diabetes, high blood pressure, peptic ulcers, and emotional illnesses—especially neurosis, psychoneurosis, psychosis, and depression—should seek medical supervision for those problems and should practice the exercises only with the medical supervisor's approval and guidance.

We would like to thank a variety of people who have contributed to the success of this book. Without the help of Meyer Friedman, Beata Jencks, Marshal Kreuter, and John Mitchel, the original program which evolved into this book would never have materialized. We thank William Chen and Gary Gilmore for comments on our very rough drafts. Our many students forced us to keep abreast of current knowledge. Kathleen Ekern typed the final manuscript. And, last and most important, we thank Kathy and Ellen, our wives, for their encouragement and constant support.

# PART ONE

# UNDERSTANDING STRESS

The individual who is about to start a stress management program needs to understand stress. Part One provides information about the physiology of stress, about stress gone bad, and about the benefits of relaxation.

*Stress gone bad* refers to the constant elicitation of the stress response, which breaks the body's internal rhythm, or equilibrium. Over a long enough time, and because of the body's adaptive mechanisms, there is a retraining of the autonomic and endocrine systems. This can lead to feelings of helplessness, frustration, desperation, and disappointment, and to stress-related illnesses—to distress.

Part One includes a look at the concepts of health, wellness, and holistic health and discusses how these relate to one another and to relaxation. Each of these terms is interpreted differently by professionals. Here we present our interpretations. These will help you to see how the various components of a stress management program fit together.

# 1

███████████████

# HEALTH AND WELLNESS: AN ELUSIVE GOAL?

While living beside Walden Pond Henry David Thoreau wrote, "The cost of a thing is the amount of life required to be exchanged for it, immediately or in the long run." This observation is as valid today as it was a hundred years ago—perhaps even more so. Many people today feel as though they are being bombarded each day with new information. The pace at which we live and the rate at which new problems develop leave us with little time to adapt to our changing society. Is it possible for us to have happy, healthful, productive lives in contemporary society? The current interest in health and in the environment suggests that many people are concerned about this question.

Recent movements in the health professions indicate an upswing in interest in several areas related to health and the environment, including wellness, holistic health, primary prevention, environmental sensitivity, physical fitness, and stress management. Several of these fields, such as wellness and holistic health, are relatively new. We need to understand what these terms mean if we are to understand stress management. How a person views health and wellness is a basic factor in how that individual approaches a total relaxation program.

We begin our discussion by examining holistic health. Health viewed in the holistic sense is integral to stress management and a total relaxation program. Furthermore, when health is viewed from the holistic viewpoint, it is easier to relate stress management to other health topics. This in turn

**3**

facilitates establishment of a stress management program through application of wellness principles.

## WHAT IS HEALTH?

Is health just an absence of disease? Or does *health* refer to the quality of life of an individual? Health means different things to different people. The life experiences of an individual determine that person's definition of health and the importance of health to that individual.[1]

In the past, health was most often defined as an absence of disease or injury. But the absence of disease or injury does not insure a healthy state. Many people without disease or injury are bored, unhappy, depressed, and alone. Are they healthy?

The current approach to defining health is more inclusive. Although professionals do not agree on one specific definition, an accepted viewpoint is that health is more than an absence of disease or injury. Some believe that health refers to the quality of life of an individual. The World Health Organization defines health as a "complete state of physical, mental, and social well-being and not merely the absence of disease or infirmity."[2] This definition describes a more desirable state than the minimum of an absence of disease or injury and implies that health is a state of being. The process of moving toward a higher level of health involves the whole person. The whole person is made up of several distinct but interrelated dimensions—the physical, mental, emotional, and spiritual aspects of the individual. These dimensions function together in a dynamic process. And so we come to the concept of holistic health.

## HOLISTIC HEALTH

We are concerned here with how the individual views or interprets health and applies health-related principles in daily living situations. Most health professionals today view health as multidimensional. Concern with the health of an individual needs to focus on that person's emotional, mental, social, spiritual, and physical well-being, because these are interrelated. Only when each of these dimensions is viewed as part of the whole can the health, or the level of health, of an individual be determined.

This is the holistic approach to health. In this approach, the whole individual is equal to the sum of his or her parts. The parts are the physical, emotional, social, mental, and spiritual dimensions of the person's being and the interaction of these with each other and with the environment.[3] The individual can be separated into these various dimensions, but each dimension must be viewed as being part of the whole.

## THE TOTAL PERSON CONCEPT

Marshall Kreuter of the University of Utah has developed a holistic approach to health, the "total person concept"[4] (see Figure 1-1). He explains that an understanding of human beings as multidimensional fosters consideration of health problems as they may affect or be affected by any one dimension or by a combination of dimensions. The total person concept asserts that each individual is composed of physical, mental, social, emotional, and spiritual dimensions. These dimensions are interrelated and interdependent in the functioning of the whole person.

Kreuter considers each of the five dimensions as a needs system, and he asserts that each dimension requires specific input from the environment if the individual is to achieve optimum, healthy development. The individual's reactions—emotionally, mentally, socially, spiritually, and physically—will be positive or negative depending on the type and degree of input received.

FIGURE 1-1

*The Total-Person Concept*

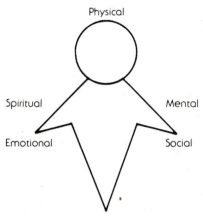

SOURCE: J. D. Curtis and R. L. Papenfuss, *Health Instruction: A Task Approach* (Minneapolis: Burgess, 1980), p. 27.

For example, if a man has taken good care of his body, his body will, theoretically, have a maximum potential for efficient functioning. If he has neglected or abused his body, that neglect or abuse is detrimental to the development of satisfactory health. Similarly, a child who is loved will be healthier and will function more effectively than a child who is rejected by his or her parents. Kreuter provides the examples of positive and negative input for each dimension presented in Table 1-1.

Accurate assessment of health problems is seriously hampered if we try to draw conclusions on the basis of observation of a single act or reaction—if we view the person as a unidimensional entity rather than as a total being with several complex dimensions. An assessment based on observation of a single dimension can lead to misleading conclusions about matters related to health. Again, an example is useful. If a woman appears anxious and impatient and has muscular tensions, doing a relaxation exercise may help her. Only the physical symptoms will be alleviated, however. Has this woman really been helped? Or has she simply been given a band-aid with which to cover the symptoms?

The physical symptoms may be the result of many things. Perhaps this woman is tense in a group of people because she has a poor self-image. Maybe she has not developed effective communication skills. If her problem is poor self-image or inability to communicate effectively, relaxation may not get to the root of the problem. Instead, it may prolong her agony by postponing an appropriate solution.

TABLE 1-1
*Positive and Negative Input*

| Dimension | Positive Input | Negative Input |
|---|---|---|
| Physical | Food, water, oxygen, exercise | Starvation, contamination, atrophy |
| Emotional | Love, trust | Hate, mistrust, anonymity |
| Mental | Ideas, knowledge | Ignorance |
| Social | Interaction with people | Seclusion, escape |
| Spiritual | Values, morality | No morality |

SOURCE: M. Kreuter, "The Five Dimensions of Man." (Paper distributed at the University of Utah, Salt Lake City, 1972).

If we use the holistic approach to health, we need to develop health maintenance, prevention, and intervention programs on the same comprehensive model. The individual who wants to become more relaxed, effective, and healthier needs to develop a holistic program. Relaxation exercises are a part of such a program.

## WELLNESS

Wellness is a concept, a value, a life style, and a process. The word *wellness*, like the word *health*, means different things to different people. You need a clear understanding of our interpretation of wellness before you start on a stress management program.

There are numerous definitions of wellness. We will define wellness here as feeling good enough about yourself to regularly take stock of (assess) your life, to intervene and to nourish yourself whenever necessary, and to find or develop the necessary reinforcement and motivation to continue your movement toward personal growth, development, and utilization of your potential. Let's examine the three key components of this operational definition of wellness.[5]

First, you regularly assess your life. Every day we are involved in making assessments. When you wake up in the morning, you assess how you feel. If you decide you feel sick, that is an assessment. When you look into the bathroom mirror, you may assess your appearance. Assessments can also be made about a specific health habit (for example, smoking), about a specific personal dimension (for example, spiritual), about strengths and weaknesses, and about the direction of your life. An assessment of wellness is deliberate and conscious and includes examining and identifying strengths and finding ways to maintain or foster those strengths. Assessment is the art of determining who you are now and comparing that to your idea of who you want to be in the future. Wellness is not experienced, however, simply because an assessment is made. Wellness is an active process that requires involvement, and that involvement is the basis for the next component.

The second key component of wellness combines intervention and nourishment. You experience wellness because of what you do to intervene and nourish. Once you have assessed who you are, you can use knowledge, habits, practices, and skills to change and to make improvements.

Let's say your assessment is that you are under too much stress because you are overcommitted. To intervene means to do something positive, in this situation to reduce or alleviate the circumstances generating the stress. The intervention may be to delegate a part of your work load to a colleague.

It may mean establishing priorities and dealing with only the top priorities. It may mean establishing a personal time period to walk, jog, read, listen to music, or perform a relaxation exercise. It may mean making a conscious effort to approach each day at a slower pace. The intervention is an action taken to help you feel better about yourself. Feeling better rejuvenates, revitalizes, and creates a fresh perspective toward life.

The second aspect of this component is nourishment, and it, too, is directed toward maximizing existing potentials. You may already be doing many positive things for yourself. It's important to continue nurturing yourself in those ways. If relaxation exercises help you to feel less anxious about certain events, or if you feel better after relaxation, then you may want to do these exercises regularly, rather than waiting until the assessment indicates a need for intervention. But it is important not to focus only on intervention. Continual nourishment and development of the positive aspects of one's life are essential for balance and well-being.

As a result of the intervention and nourishment, growth occurs and higher levels of health are experienced. Since the growth is determined by assessment, intervention, and nourishment, even a setback can result in growth and wellness if you learn about yourself from it. You can use a setback to reassess and begin anew. When you view the wellness process this way, your self-concept is not tarnished by defeat. We have all, at some time, felt defeated during a jogging program, a diet attempt, an effort to improve communication skills or restructure a belief system. But it is only when we stop trying, assessing, and working on intervention and nourishment that we are defeated.

The third key component of our operational definition of wellness is reinforcement and motivation. Positive reinforcement is a most effective motivator of continued effort. Reinforcement is crucial in any health practice. In the beginning, reinforcement is usually observable and measurable. It is losing two pounds on a diet; it is seeing the dollars and cents saved after giving up an undesirable habit such as smoking; it is finally building enough endurance to walk or jog a mile; or it is having fewer disagreements with your spouse after striving to improve communication skills. These are important reinforcers in the initial phases of experiencing and practicing wellness, but they are often not enough to motivate continued efforts. What is?

Motivation is one of the most difficult problems facing those in the field of health. Basic principles of health, such as diet, weight control, physical fitness, and relaxation are relatively simple to learn. But how does an individual become motivated to incorporate the principles into his or her daily life? Many people are motivated by the results they obtain from regular practice of relaxation exercises. If you find, after you have begun to practice the exercises, that you have fewer and less severe headaches, if you are able to fall asleep more easily and to sleep more soundly, if you feel less hurried and tense, then you will be motivated to continue practicing relaxation.

Perhaps the greatest reinforcement a person can receive is positive feelings. The interventions you make and the nourishing things that you do to make yourself feel better are reinforcing. If you feel better because of assessment and actions taken, you are likely to continue. Feelings are genuine. They last, have an impact, and help improve self-concept. The strongest motivation to continue interventions and nourishing activities is the positive feelings received from those efforts. Wellness is feeling good enough about yourself to regularly take stock of your life, to intervene and to nourish whenever and wherever possible, and to find or develop reinforcements and motivations to continue.

Wellness is a life style that is positively and consciously directed toward maintaining balance within oneself and with the external environment. Wellness is a life style characterized by self-expression and satisfaction. It is a way of living and a way of growing. It is a self-determined value for those who choose it as a way of experiencing life. Human beings value many things, however, so we need to put this in proper perspective.

In *Values and Teaching*, Louis Raths, Merrill Harmin, and Sidney Simon[6] discuss criteria for values. These criteria are useful in examining your own values:

1. A value is chosen freely. No one forces it on you. If you adopt a wellness life style, you have decided of your own accord to experience wellness.

2. You choose a value freely, after considering various alternatives and thinking about the consequences of adopting each. After considering, perhaps even experiencing, various values, you choose the ones that are best for you.

3. You prize and cherish a value. It is important enough to you so that you are willing to defend it against criticism, and you want to keep it as part of your life.

4. You publicly affirm your belief in the value you have chosen. And you want, in your practice of that value, to be a positive example for others to emulate. Remember that others may not accept your value — we are all different and have different values.

5. You live according to your values, as consistently as you are able to. As you grow and change, you need to reassess your values. This will enable you to continue to live according to your values, without experiencing conflict between old values and new ones.

Wellness involves the total person. You take your whole being everywhere you go and into every life experience. Each dimension of the total person is affected by life experiences. The individual who adopts wellness as a value develops each dimension and finds ways to express wholeness to others.

Wellness is a process.[7] It is ongoing. If you expect miracles to occur overnight, you will be disappointed. Change and growth are slow processes. The important thing is that you have become more committed to and more involved with your life. This brings us to the cornerstone of the wellness process—self-responsibility.

The glue that unifies the values, life style, and process of wellness into a cohesive and exciting approach to living is self-responsibility. Wellness is a process that you do alone, but with reinforcement, motivation, knowledge, and skills received from others. It is a process that is started, maintained, directed, and redirected by you. As hard as some people try, no one can buy health, well-being, or happiness. No one can steal any of these from someone else, and no one can afford the luxury of sitting back and waiting for them to happen. The process of achieving these requires action, effort, and involvement, by you and for you.

Expressing both the motivational and self-responsibility components of wellness, John Pilch has stated that "motivation for wellness must be rooted in conversion; that is, a change of outlook. Conversion in this sense is both a process and an event. The process begins with awareness and continues with increasing awareness. Then, at some point, conversion takes place. A person decides to quit a high-paying but frustrating job in preference for one with a lower salary but increased satisfaction; a chain smoker finally decides to quit smoking."[8] The process, the event, can be influenced by others. But the conversion, the decision to take action, comes from within. If you expect someone or something to do it for you, you do not experience wellness. Wellness is experienced when you can say, "I'm doing it for myself."

## Wellness and Growth

Each person grows, chronologically and in maturity. The wellness process is part of the maturation process. Most sickness–health continuums and wellness continuums have been pictured as horizontal. We believe that growth in the wellness framework, including all human dimensions, is a vertical process—the wellness process focuses on the achievement of higher levels of health, wellness, and maturation.

Figure 1-2 depicts growth as a vertical process. Growth reaches, moves, sometimes struggles, upward. What about setbacks, roadblocks, and

FIGURE 1-2
*The Wellness Process*

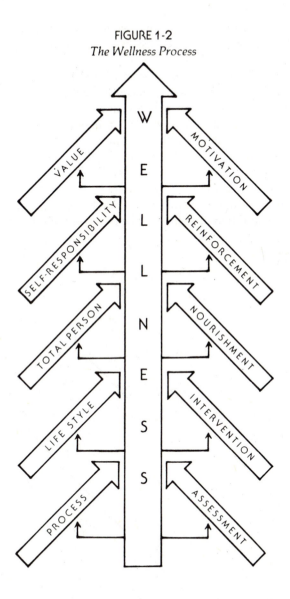

failures? In the wellness process, they can lead to change and growth. They are factors in assessments and reassessments, in decisions to take particular actions, in the individual's developing sense of responsibility and commitment. Frustrations and disappointments can be among our most beneficial experiences, if we learn from them and use what we learn. They eventually lead to the greatest growth and utilization of our human potentials. In Figure

1-2, the arrows on the vertical plane would turn downward only if the individual had given up, stopped assessing, stopped trying to achieve a healthier life.

Pilch views the wellness process in yet another way. He sees wellness as a line parallel to the sickness–health continuum, rather than an extension of it. Pilch believes that wellness includes having a purpose in life, identifying life's true pleasures and joys, accepting the responsibility for free self-determination, and finding effective and lasting motivation. According to this definition, a person could be terminally ill, mentally handicapped, or permanently disabled, and still have a high level of wellness. On the other hand, a person could be reasonably healthy by accepted medical standards but have no purpose in living and so would not be experiencing wellness.[9] It is possible to be at different points on the two continuums, as noted in Figure 1-3.

FIGURE 1-3

*Health versus Wellness*

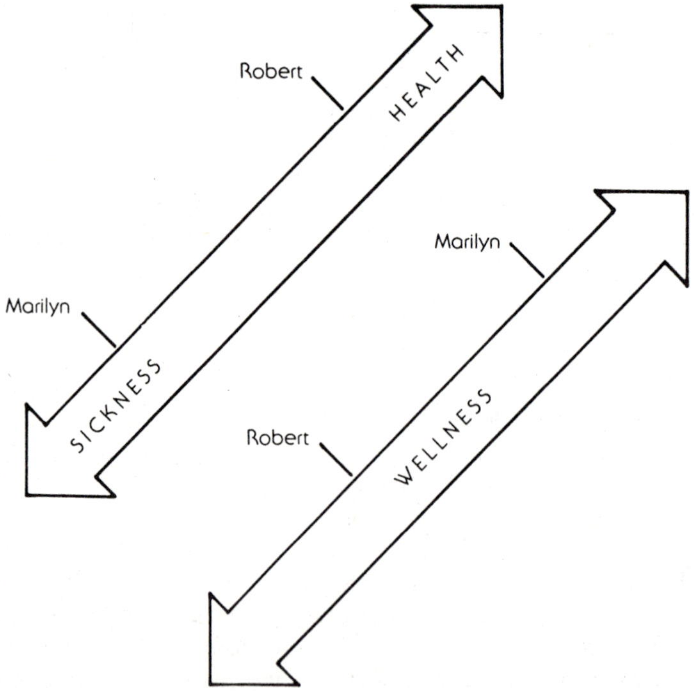

Look around you at those you know well. Perhaps you have known people like Robert and Marilyn. Robert outwardly appeared to be above average on the sickness–health continuum. He was symptom free—he had no apparent physical complaints or ills and was able to function fairly well in his chosen life style  However, Robert found no purpose or meaning in life. He was an adopted child and had struggled to understand and accept that. He had difficulty establishing interpersonal relationships. College was difficult for him, not because of a lack of intelligence but because he lacked direction and was unable to decide on a career that would be fulfilling and satisfying. He finally chose a career, but as time passed, Robert became unhappy in this career and with himself as a person. His assessments and his efforts to become a better person and maximize his potentials were minimal. Unable to effectively bring about positive changes in his life, Robert felt immobilized and stagnant. This, in turn, precipitated more unhappiness. At the age of forty-six he had a severe heart attack. During and after convalescence he was, still, unable to change his life. Overwhelmed by dissatisfaction as well as other stresses, he had a second heart attack and died when he was forty-eight. His life experience does not exemplify wellness.

Now let's look at Marilyn. Marilyn is married and has five children whose ages range from eleven to twenty-three. Ten months ago, Marilyn discovered that she had terminal cancer. She is forty-two years old and in the prime of life. Before the cancer developed, she was full of energy, excited about life, alive. After going through the process of grieving over having only a year to live and adjusting to that diagnosis, Marilyn reevaluated her life. Each day now has a special meaning, a special purpose. She even makes better use of her time. She radiates strength and courage to those around her as she continues to live those remaining months and days to the fullest of her existing potentials. Even on the days when she can no longer get out of bed, her body wracked with pain, she smiles and tries to help those around her to be more at peace with what is happening. Her major purpose after months of suffering has been to provide and experience one more Christmas with her family. The greatest gifts at Christmas are not found in packages, but in the gift of life and in the specialness that being together can bring. Even during the months when Marilyn had a terminal illness, she experienced wellness.

Can you put another name to Marilyn? Is there a mother, a father, a neighbor in your life who has had a similar illness and a similar attitude? Many people who are not symptom free experience wellness. They experience life as fully as they can—they are involved in the wellness process. In their special ways, they are growing. It is possible to "be terminally ill, mentally retarded, or permanently disabled, yet have a keen sense of life's purpose and deep appreciation of the joy of living and therefore have a high level of wellness, though your health may never improve."[10]

The wellness process allows growth to occur in a person's own set of circumstances. Change and growth for each of us is very personal. As you continue to grow, you become aware that you don't ever arrive at wellness. You realize that it is the experiencing of the process that counts. Are you ready to experience, to make the commitment, and to become more involved with your life?

## The Wellness Wheel

The major areas of focus for increased well-being are emotional/mental stability, physical fitness, nutrition, and stress management. Throughout the country programs are surfacing that focus on enhancing well-being in each of these major areas. They are certainly prime areas of concern for contemporary women and men. Figure 1-4 is the Wellness Wheel, which includes all of these areas as the spokes of a wheel whose hub is commitment to health. The spokes and the hub provide strength and balance that enable the individual's

FIGURE 1-4
*The Wellness Wheel*

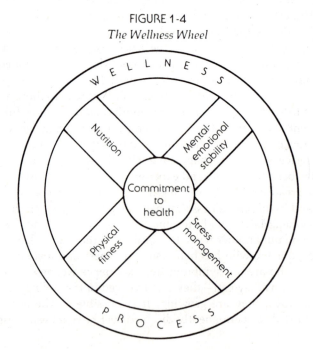

wellness process to function—so that the individual can handle the rough terrain of failures and setbacks and keep on rolling. A reasonable amount of positive input (as described by Kreuter and personally assessed), self-responsibility, and motivation are needed to stay on the path of wellness.

Stress management is but one of many components of a wellness approach to living. All of the areas of health are important. If a wellness program is to be effective, an individual must have a holistic approach to life, dealing with the total person and all health areas—including stress management and relaxation.

### Wellness and Relaxation

If an individual has a holistic or multidimensional view of life and focuses on wellness rather than simply avoiding injury or disease, all health programs engaged in should reflect these beliefs. A stress management program should be part of a comprehensive health program, and the stress program itself should be comprehensive.

A comprehensive stress management program must meet the needs of the individual in all five dimensions (physical, emotional, mental, social, and spiritual). Such a program includes all aspects of stress management: (1) recognizing stress and identifying the source of stress (assessment); (2) developing sensory awareness—identifying tensions when they first appear; (3) identifying inappropriate stress responses and controlling these responses—recognizing that stress is not detrimental, but that accumulated stress responses are detrimental; and (4) learning how to relax when tension is inappropriate and undesirable, using the total relaxation approach discussed in this book.

Many relaxation programs focus only on the last component—how to relax. Too often these programs teach one or two relaxation methods and fail to provide a comprehensive approach to stress management. Participants in such programs often experience failure and stop regular practicing after a short time. A comprehensive approach, which includes early intervention in the stress cycle and the use of relaxation exercises to nourish the body, mind, and spirit, is essential.

### SUMMARY

Important to a holistic relaxation program is coming to an understanding of health and wellness. Since a person's total being is taken into every life experience, the total person needs to be considered when defining health and wellness. Each dimension (physical, mental, social, emotional, spiritual) has various needs. When these needs are met, chances for improving health are increased.

Similar to yet distinct from "health" is *wellness*. Wellness is a process that encourages the individual to examine and become more actively involved with life. Major components of this process are assessment, intervention and nourishment, and reinforcement and motivation. Wellness is also a life style and a value. The individual assumes responsibility for starting the process of change and growth, maintaining it, and, when necessary, redirecting it. It is possible to be healthy by accepted medical standards while not experiencing a high degree of wellness. It is also possible for a person to experience wellness while permanently disabled, handicapped, or terminally ill.

The four areas in which the wellness process has great potential for increasing health and well-being are emotional/mental stability, physical fitness, nutrition, and stress management. A comprehensive stress management program encompasses the total person. One vital component of a stress management program is the art of relaxation, which is used as an intervention strategy.

Other strategies include recognizing stress and the sources of stress, identifying when a reaction to a stressor may be inappropriate and may have detrimental effects on health, and developing an awareness of tension. Any attempt to reduce and control stress must be comprehensive and must include all dimensions of the total person.

### Notes

1 John D. Curtis and Richard L. Papenfuss, *Health Instruction: A Task Approach* (Minneapolis: Burgess, 1980), p. 14.

2 John Hanlon, as cited in *Public Health: Administration and Practice* (St. Louis: C. V. Mosby, 1974), p. 53.

3 Kenneth R. Pelletier, *Mind as Healer, Mind as Slayer: A Holistic Approach to Preventing Stress Disorders* (New York: Dell, 1977), p. 11.

4 Marshall Kreuter, "The Five Dimensions of Man" (Paper distributed at the University of Utah, Salt Lake City, 1972).

5 Gary D. Gilmore, "Planning for Family Wellness," *Health Education* 10 (1979): 12–16.

6 L. Raths, M. Harmin, and S. Simon, *Values and Teaching* (Columbus: Charles E. Merrill, 1966).

7 John G. Bruhn, David F. Cordova, James A. Williams, and Raymond G. Fuentes, Jr., "The Wellness Process," *Journal of Community Health* 2 (1977): 209–221.

8 John Pilch, "Wellness: What Is It and How Can We Get It?" *Health Review* (1979): 19.

9 Ibid., pp. 16–19.
10 Ibid., p. 16.

## References

Ardell, Donald B. *High Level Wellness: An Alternative to Doctors, Drugs, and* ⸲ Emmaus, Pa.: Rodale Press, 1977.

Bruhn, John G.; Cordova, David F.; Williams, James A.; and Fuentes, Raymond G. "The Wellness Process." *Journal of Community Health* 2: 209–221.

Curtis, John D., and Papenfuss, Richard L. *Health Instruction: A Task Approach.* Minneapolis: Burgess, 1980.

Dunn, Halbert L. *High-Level Wellness.* Arlington, Va.: R. W. Beatty, 1973.

Gilmore, Gary D. "Planning for Family Wellness." *Health Education* 10 (1979): 12–16.

Hanlon, John. *Public Health: Administration and Practice.* St. Louis: C. V. Mosby, 1974.

Kreuter, Marshall. "The Five Dimensions of Man." Paper distributed at the University of Utah, Salt Lake City, 1972.

Pelletier, Kenneth R. *Mind as Healer, Mind as Slayer.* New York: Dell, 1977.

Pilch, John. "Wellness: What Is It and How Can We Get It?" *Health Review* (1979): 19.

Raths, L.; Harmin, M.; and Simon, S. *Values and Teaching.* Columbus: Charles E. Merrill, 1966.

# 2

**██████████████**

# UNDERSTANDING STRESS

In recent years there has been a resurgence of interest in health, wellness, and the role of stress management in a holistic approach to achieving higher levels of health and wellness. Experts from many fields have written about stress management. Each definition of stress reflects the writer's area of expertise. Among those who have written about stress are medical doctors, physiologists, researchers, journalists, and educators. From their work we can learn much about stress—its characteristic causes and symptoms and the effects stress has on biological systems. And we can learn how to manage stress. If we are to effectively manage sources of stress and keep stress working for us rather than against us, each of us needs to understand what is meant by stress and the stress process.

## WHAT IS STRESS?

We should first recognize that stress is positive and is both desirable and necessary—that's right, desirable and necessary! Stress is an innate response to help us adjust to the demands of life. Don Ardell recently stated that being without stress "would be like going to a party on Friday night and spending the evening in the closet with the coats."[1] Hans Selye, a doctor and a pioneer in the area of stress and stress-related research, has suggested that stress is the "spice of life," that to be without stress means to be without life.[2]

We may describe stress as a series of normal body reactions necessary for self-preservation. Each second that we are alive our bodies are reacting to various demands that call for adaptation or adjustment. Normal body reactions help us to respond to internal and external environmental forces. These responses aid us in maintaining body balance or in returning our bodies to a balanced state should our equilibrium be upset. The body's normal state of being in equilibrium is referred to as *homeostasis*. The concept of homeostasis was originally proposed by French physiologist Claude Bernard, who taught "that one of the most characteristic features of all living beings is their ability to maintain the constancy of their internal milieu, despite changes in the surroundings."[3] Walter B. Cannon, a Harvard physiologist, labeled this self-regulating system in living beings as homeostasis in 1932. It is the ability to remain the same, and in a layman's sense it is "staying power."

## COMPONENTS OF STRESS

Stress can be thought of as the interrelationship between the stressor (the cause) and the stress response (the effect). We will discuss these two components of stress in the order that they occur—first stressors and then the stress responses, or reactions to the stressors.

### Stressors

A stressor is a demand, situation, or circumstance that disrupts an individual's equilibrium and initiates the stress response. A stressor is to the body as a trigger is to a gun. As the trigger of a gun is squeezed (a demand is placed on it), a series of events is initiated. In a gun, the firing pin is propelled into the shell where a small explosion occurs that generates pressure in a confined space and results in the release of the bullet from the shell. Released from the confines of the holding chamber, the bullet speeds toward its target. In a similar manner, the stressor (demand) activates a series of events within the body. Chemicals, hormones, and neural impulses are fired within seconds or fractions of a second after activation. This is the stress response.

**Types of Stressors**   There are many different kinds of stressors. Life is full of them, and it is perfectly normal for a person to encounter many stressors each day. There are big stressors, little stressors, nagging stressors, acute stressors, and unidentified stressors. For most of us, the stressor that is most readily perceived is usually the one that acts as "the straw that breaks the camel's back" and initiates the stress response. We usually are not fully aware of the variety of daily stressors that eventually accumulate and trigger the stress response. We are aware of big events or demands that call for a great deal of adjustment or adaptation and small stressors that carry us over the brink.

The demands and the responses to these demands are complex, and there are a variety of stressors working together at any time. Stressors can be grouped into five categories, presented below. As you reach each category and the examples presented, try to identify situations in your life in which these stressors generated tension, nervousness, or anxiety within your body.

1. social stressors—noise, crowding
2. psychological stressors—anxiety, worry
3. psychosocial stressors—loss of a job, death of a spouse or friend
4. biochemical stressors—heat, cold, injury, pollutants, toxicants, poor nutrition
5. philosophical stressors—value system conflict, lack of purpose, lack of direction

The environment contains numerous potential triggers or demands. Can you identify stressors that have made you feel tense, nervous, or anxious? In what category do they belong? Are they single events or combinations of events? Remember that stressors, individually or in combination, are the triggers of the stress response.

**Primary versus Secondary Stressors**   A primary stressor is one that initiates the stress response. Secondary stressors are events that result from the first stressor and keep the stress response activated. Often this creates a vicious cycle that continues to trigger the stress response.

To understand the primary-secondary stress cycle, consider the situation in which a wage earner has been fired from a job (primary stressor). Emotions such as frustration and anger elicit the stress response that facilitates adjustment. Then worry (as a secondary stressor) is likely to begin— "How will I support my family, pay bills?" It may also be expressed as concern about what "I" did wrong, where "I" went astray—as self-blame. Worry is a special kind of stressor. It raises anxiety levels and keeps the stress response activated long after the primary stressor initially activated that response. The individual who begins to consume alcohol as a means of coping adds another secondary stressor. If this person also becomes apathetic and depressed, the apathy and depression are additional secondary stressors. All of these secondary stressors keep the stress response activated. It is easy to see how an individual's life can quickly get out of control because of this cycle.

Stimulus overload in one's job is another primary stressor that occurs when there is too much to be done and not enough time in which to do everything. Many people move frantically from one task to another and soon find that this has elicited the stress response. Do you know people who have "hurry sickness"—a constant sense of "time urgency?" If the individual continues to worry about meeting deadlines and getting tasks done, the stress response may continue to be elicited, especially if the worry is carried from the job into the family setting. When this cycle is constantly elicited, it can eventually lead to ulcers. It is important to be aware of how the primary-secondary stress cycle works and to note that it is not an isolated single event but a combination of stressors that keeps the stress response activated. The particular combination of primary and secondary stressors is unique to each person—to his or her life events and perceptions of those life events.

**Perception of the Stressor**  Although the external environment contains many potential stressors for each of us in our day-to-day lives, not all of us will react, adjust, or elicit the stress response to the same stressors. What is a stressor for one person may not be a stressor for another. As Hans Selye has pointed out many times, "It is not the stressor that is important, but how one takes the stressor."

Each of us "takes" or perceives stressors differently. Why? How can an event or experience be a stressor for one person but not for another? Each person has a unique personality, life experience, socialization, and set of values. All of these are factors in determining how a particular person perceives a particular event and, thus, how that person responds to that event. The individual who has a positive self-concept and has experienced success in many areas of life is likely to perceive stress as a challenge. The individual who has a negative self-concept and has experienced failure is likely to perceive stress as a threat. Past experience will influence present perceptions, perhaps as much as or more than the nature and intensity of the stressor.

## Physiology of the Stress Response

Each of us has been aware of the outward signals of the stress response when we have been frightened. These bodily responses also are likely to be experienced when a close friend or relative dies, when we lose a job, or even when we get married. In fact, any event that causes us to adapt or change will elicit similar signs. The common, identifiable signals include increased heartbeat, increased respiratory rate, increased perspiration, increased muscular tension, dry mouth, and a general overall increase in body metabolism. These, however, are only the external manifestations of the total stress response. The response pathways are extremely complex and involve the body's entire physiological response to internal and external environmental factors. Our attempt here is to provide a very simplistic overview of this physiology, so that you can understand what happens as the stress response is initiated.

The human brain is more complicated than the most complex computer. It is capable of simultaneously sending and receiving millions of messages from the senses. When we encounter a situation (stressor) that requires change or adaptation, the higher centers of the brain (the cerebral cortex) receive a message. The switchboard for the millions of incoming and outgoing messages is a part of the brain called the thalamus. The thalamus is responsible for sorting information and transferring it to the cerebral cortex. This switchboard is necessary to keep us from reacting in a hundred different ways at one time. As a stressful situation is perceived, another area of the brain, the hypothalamus, is stimulated. Now the action really begins, because once the hypothalamus is activated, the two major response pathways (see Figures 2-1 and 2-2) are called into play.

**Endocrine System**  One pathway involves normal reactions through the endocrine system (Figure 2-1). As the hypothalamus is stimulated, the anterior portion of this gland releases a hormone called the corticotrophin releasing factor (CRF). The function of the CRF is to activate a part of the pituitary gland so that it releases another hormone, adrenocorticotrophin hormone (ACTH), into general body circulation. An intermediate hormone, ACTH stimulates the target organ, the adrenal cortex. (Small amounts of ACTH are being released from the pituitary gland at all times, although the exact level may vary according to the time of day. When we are exposed to a mental or physical demand, the pituitary gland can promote a release of up to twenty times the normal basal output. This hormonal output will be in general circulation within just seconds after the demand has been placed on the body. Some of the demands that elicit this series of reactions are trauma, heat, cold, restraint, and surgery.[4] (The two primary secretions of the adrenal cortex are the gluco-corticoids (primary cortisol) and the mineralo-corticoids (primarily aldosterone).[5]

Once the cortisol is in circulation, needed metabolic alterations occur. Now the body attempts to get as much glucose (sugar) into circulation as is needed to cope with the demand and to bring relief as the body adjusts to that demand. As relief occurs, the cortisol acts to shut down the production of CRF in the hypothalamus. The aldosterone is transported by the blood and

FIGURE 2-1

*The Stress Response: Endocrine Involvement*

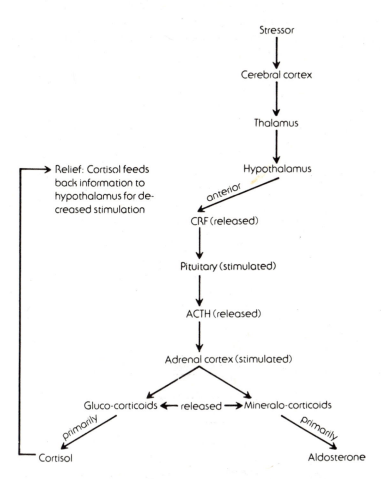

acts on the kidney to increase the amount of sodium (salt) reabsorbed; that is, there is a decreased amount of sodium excreted in the urine. There is an increased osmotic pressure, which forces fluid from the extracellular spaces into the blood. This results in increased blood volume and thus in increased blood pressure.[6] All of this physiology is part of a remarkable system of checks and balances within the body.

**Autonomic Nervous System**   The second major physiological pathway involves the autonomic nervous system (Figure 2-2). The autonomic nervous system regulates bodily functions not normally controlled voluntarily (heart rate, respiratory rate, and glandular secretions), and it is made up of the sympathetic and parasympathetic components. These two components act to balance each other. The sympathetic component is responsible for energy

FIGURE 2-2

*The Stress Response:*
*Autonomic Nervous System Involvement*

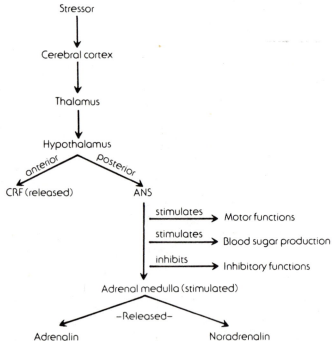

Stressor

↓

Cerebral cortex

↓

Thalamus

↓

Hypothalamus

*anterior*      *posterior*

CRF (released)            ANS

stimulates → Motor functions

stimulates → Blood sugar production

inhibits → Inhibitory functions

Adrenal medulla (stimulated)

–Released–

| Adrenalin | Noradrenalin |
|---|---|
| • increases carbohydrate metabolism | • increases systolic and diastolic blood pressure |
| • dilates arterials in heart and skeletal muscles | • increases frequency and strength of heartbeat |
| • accelerates heart rate and increases volume of blood | |
| • elevates body temperature | |
| • increase $O_2$ consumption | |
| • relaxes smooth muscles of gut | |
| • dilates musculature | |

expenditure (elevated heart rate), while the parasympathetic is concerned with energy conservation (depressed heart rate).[7] In the stress response, the autonomic nervous system (ANS) works as follows.

As the anterior portion of the hypothalamus is busy releasing CRF, the posterior hypothalamus is busy exciting or inhibiting other bodily functions. One of the major targets of the sympathetic stimulation is the adrenal medulla. When the medulla is stimulated, the hormones adrenalin and noradrenalin are released. These two action-preparation hormones are responsible for the quick surge of strength that readies the body for fight or flight. It is the rush of these action hormones into circulation that is responsible for the remarkable feats accomplished in emergency situations. The action of these hormones on carbohydrate and fat metabolism and on the cardiovascular system enables each of us to meet demands—especially demands that involve survival or severe stress. The demands most likely to trigger the ANS and adrenalin and noradrenalin into action are fear, severe pain, anger, and any situation that threatens physical harm.[8]

The autonomic nervous system serves other vital functions to help meet the demands placed on the body. One of these is to stimulate motor functioning. Once the ANS is stimulated, the following happens:

1. Heart muscles dilate (enlarge) and there is increased stroke volume of the heart and increased cardiac output.
2. The spleen constricts to release stored blood so that, with the increased cardiac output, more oxygen is available for use within the body.
3. Blood vessels in the skeletal muscles are dilated and, with the increased muscular tension and metabolic rate, the increased oxygen is utilized.
4. Blood pressure increases.
5. The pupils of the eyes dilate.
6. The pilomotor muscles constrict (causing goose bumps and making the hair stand on end).
7. Increased output from the sweat glands and the salivary glands produces a thick saliva that we recognize as "dry mouth" or "cotton mouth."

Each of us has noticed these signals when we have encountered stressful situations. Other vital reactions that take place are not as easily noticed but are important in meeting demands. These are the inhibitory functions of the ANS, which include:

1. Blood flow to vital organs is redistributed.

2. Stomach and urinary bladder muscles relax (stop contracting).
3. The walls of the bronchioles (the tiny air passages within the lungs) relax making it easier for air to get into and out of the lungs.

Another important change that is part of the stress response is decrease in blood clotting time. One of the major mechanisms for survival is the clotting of blood. The constriction of blood vessels in the skin and viscera and the redistribution of blood throughout the body are accompanied by an increase of coagulants in the blood. The result is that bleeding stops more rapidly if injuries are received during a stressful confrontation. Whether injuries actually result or not, when a person is under stress, blood clotting time decreases.

It is the hypothalamus, with its intimate relationship to the pituitary gland, that provides the link between the nervous system and the endocrine system. In responding to stress, these systems work in coordination with each other. Working together, they are "the stress reaction." The human body and mind are truly remarkable, and so is this process by which the body maintains or regains balance. Inability to meet demands or restore body balance would eventually result in death. The stress response, then, is responsible for our aliveness, enjoyment, and survival—it is vital for life!

## SUMMARY

To be alive is to have some stress. It is the body's normal reaction for self-preservation and so is a necessary part of life. Stress reactions occur through the autonomatic nervous and endocrine pathways. The most identifiable signals of the normal response include increased heart and respiratory rates, increased muscular tension and perspiration, and dry mouth.

The demands that elicit the stress response are called stressors. Almost everything encountered in life has the potential to be a stressor. There are social stressors, psychological stressors, psychosocial stressors, biochemical stressors, and philosophical stressors. Anything that triggers the stress response is a stressor. A primary stressor is the original demand that elicits the response. A secondary stressor is one that keeps the response activated beyond the point when the body would normally return to homeostasis. Disappointment, frustration, anger, and worry are examples of secondary stressors that can feed primary-secondary stress cycles and keep the response elicited.

What is a stressor for one person may not be a stressor for another. Factors that influence how we respond to stressors include perception, past behavioral adjustment patterns, and overall ability to cope.

## Notes

1 Donald B. Ardell, "Whole Person Excelience: The Wellness Lifestyle" (speech presented at the University of Wisconsin–La Crosse, 1979).

2 Hans Selye, *Stress Without Distress* (New York: Signet, New American Library, 1974), p. 83.

3 Hans Selye, *The Stress of Life* (New York: McGraw-Hill, 1976) p. 12.

4 William Chen, "Stress and Disease—Adrenal Gland" (paper distributed at the University of Wisconsin–La Crosse, 1977).

5 Daniel A. Girdano and George S. Everly, *Controlling Stress and Tension: A Holistic Approach* (Englewood Cliffs, N. J.: Prentice-Hall, 1979), p. 36.

6 D. W. Edington and V. R. Edgerton, *The Biology of Physical Activity* (Boston: Houghton Mifflin, 1976), p. 185.

7 Ibid., p. 82.

8 Kenneth R. Pelletier, *Mind as Healer, Mind as Slayer: A Holistic Approach to Preventing Stress Disorders* (New York: Dell, 1977), p. 62; Walter McQuade and Ann Aikman, *Stress: What It Is, What It Can Do to Your Health, How to Fight Back* (New York: Bantam, 1974), p. 108.

## References

Girdano, Daniel A., and Everly, George S. *Controlling Stress and Tension: A Holistic Approach.* Englewood Cliffs, N. J.: Prentice-Hall, 1979.

Greenfield, Norman S., and Sternbach, Richard A., eds. *Handbook of Psychophysiology.* New York: Holt, Rinehart and Winston, 1972.

McQuade, Walter, and Aikman, Ann. *Stress: What It Is, What It Can Do to Your Health, How to Fight Back.* New York: Bantam, 1974.

Pelletier, Kenneth R. *Mind as Healer, Mind as Slayer: A Holistic Approach to Preventing Stress Disorders.* New York: Dell, 1977.

Selye, Hans. *The Stress of Life.* New York: McGraw-Hill, 1976.

Selye, Hans. *Stress Without Distress.* New York: Signet, The New American Library, 1974.

White, John, and Fadiman, James, eds. *Relax: How You Can Feel Better, Reduce Stress, and Overcome Tension.* New York: Confucian Press, 1976.

# THE PROBLEM
# WITH STRESS

The human body is a remarkable and durable machine. All the cells, tissues, organs, and organ systems are designed to maintain balance and a healthy condition. The stress response occurs when the body's mechanisms for maintaining equilibrium and adjusting to demands are activated.

The stress response in primitive human beings was the innate response that helped them to fight or flee from danger and so to survive. Today we possess basically the same survival mechanisms, but only rarely do we find ourselves in life-threatening situations. Instead, we are beseiged by the stresses of life in modern society. The car won't start, the lines at the bank and the post office and the grocery store are long, work is tedious, a co-worker is uncooperative, a salesperson is rude, prices are up and incomes are not, the air is smoggy, the parks and highways are crowded, and we are running out of places to put human and industrial wastes. The stresses are both petty and global, and they all require behavioral adjustments.

## STRESS GONE BAD

Appropriate elicitation of the stress response does not cause problems but simply enables us to deal positively with stress. Inappropriate elicitation of the stress response—responses triggered too frequently in a short period of time or constantly over a longer period of time—can cause problems and can lead to the condition we call "stress gone bad."

Each of us has a baseline of tolerable stress (Figure 3-1). These limits are defined by the individual's genetic makeup, environment, and perceptions of life events. If we function within these limits, there seems to be no serious impairment to a balanced state. Hans Selye suggests that this is one reason why it is important for each of us to be aware of our limits. Are you a racehorse, able to tolerate many stressors in rapid succession? Or are you a turtle who needs to function at a slower pace? This assessment is crucial in stress management. If tolerance level and activity level have not been synchronized, intervention, reinforcement, and motivation for change are needed.

If our perception of an event or situation causes us to overreact, then the response is inappropriate. It is inappropriate because the fight-or-flight response may be intensified with each exposure and reaction to a stressor. A primary-secondary stress cycle is initiated, stress hormones accumulate, and the body does not have a satisfactory way to rid itself of the byproducts secreted during the elicitation. When this type of response is triggered over a prolonged period, the stress level rises and in time leads to illness, a stress-related disease, and lowered body resistance.

FIGURE 3-1

*Stress Gone Bad*

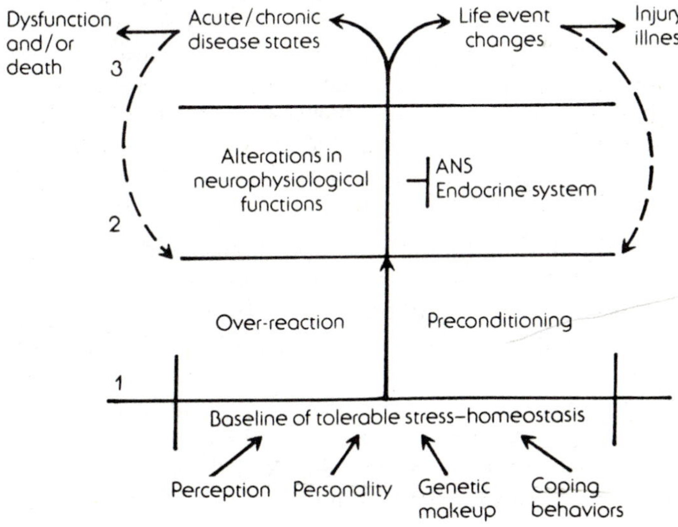

When primitive human beings were confronted with life-threatening events, such as coming face to face with a tiger, the stress response was immediately triggered, mobilizing body resources to fight the tiger or to take flight. The response was appropriate—it helped primitive human beings make the adjustments necessary for survival. No matter which choice was made, fight or flight, the body immediately exerted itself in physical activity that helped burn up excess adrenalin and noradrenalin and prevented accumulation of the byproducts of the stress response. Animals have this same response as a protective mechanism. But after the confrontation and elicitation of the fear instinct (stress response), an animal's metabolic processes quickly return to normal.

## PAPER TIGERS

Our contemporary environment is complex and change is more rapid today than ever before. Alvin Toffler has written:

> The culture shock phenomenon accounts for much of the bewilder-
> ment, frustration, and disorientation that plagues Americans in their
> dealings with other societies. It causes a breakdown in communica-
> tion, a misreading of reality, an inability to cope. Yet culture shock
> is relatively mild in comparison with the much more serious malady,
> future shock. Future shock is the dizzying disorientation brought on
> by the premature arrival of the future. It may well be the most im-
> portant disease of tomorrow. . . . unless intelligent steps are taken
> to combat it, millions of human beings will find themselves increas-
> ingly disoriented, progressively incompetent to deal rationally with
> their environments. The malaise, mass neurosis, irrationality, and
> free-floating violence already apparent in contemporary life are
> merely a foretaste of what may lie ahead unless we come to under-
> stand and treat this disease.[1]

But people have always been faced with change, and each generation has had to adjust to greater changes than the previous one. Change, then, is not totally responsible for the inappropriate elicitation of the stress response in modern human beings. At least partly responsible for the inappropriate elicitation of the response are the paper tigers that confront us—the modern-day stressors where neither fighting or fleeing is a helpful behavioral adjustment. Rapid change in social norms, mores, and cultural and other standards of conduct make adjustment difficult. And the events are not life-threatening ones but instead are confrontations with our boss or spouse, problems with marriage, divorce, promotion, deadlines, and so on. The event to be coped with may be desirable or undesirable, large or small, real or imaginary. It makes no difference to the cerebral cortex, thalamus, hypothalamus, pituitary, or adrenal glands whether or not the tigers are real. If an individual perceives an event as threatening and then overreacts, or if an individual simply encounters too many stressful events in a short period of time, the stress response will be elicited and can become inappropriate.

The stress response in modern human beings is usually not followed by physical exertion that would help rid the body of the harmful byproducts of the stress response. After all, it is not acceptable to physically attack your boss during a heated argument, nor is it acceptable to flee from a responsibility when that flight may produce another stressor—loss of your job. This is especially true if the stressor is in the form of worry, a common modern stress for which there is no satisfactory outlet. A worrier faces paper tiger after paper tiger, and the stress response is elicited over and over and over. When this happens, the individual loses control over his or her environment and over the stress response. The essence of "stress gone bad" is described by Adrian M. Ostfeld and Richard B. Shekelle: "Contemporary man in much of the world is faced every day with people and with situations about which there is uncertainty of outcome, where appropriate behavior is not prescribed and validated by tradition, where the possibility of bodily or psychological harm exists, where running or fighting is inappropriate, and where mental vigilance is called for."[2]

## STRESS AND DISEASE

The major problem created by stress gone bad is the imbalance generated within the body. When this imbalance continues or occurs repeatedly, the autonomic nervous system (ANS) and endocrine pathways are altered. Stress retrains these systems so that they no longer maintain homeostasis.[3] These changes create an internal environment in which a vital organ or system becomes susceptible to an acute or chronic disease state. Because of these changes stress-related diseases have been dubbed "diseases of adaptation."

A disease of adaptation develops when the stress level rises due to preconditioned responses or overreaction based on the individual's perception of the stressor. The alterations in the autonomic nervous system and endocrine pathways are the body's ways of adapting to the stressor. Eventually, a target organ or system may be affected. The saying "the germ is nothing, the terrain is everything" may be applicable not only to the germ theory of disease but also to stress-related diseases.

Personality plays an important role in an individual's reaction to stressors. There is much evidence to support the hypothesis that there are general personality profiles that relate to certain types of disease conditions. In other words, a person's personality may be partly responsible for determining which body system or organ is affected by constant, inappropriate elicitation of the stress response.

One of the first noteworthy studies attempting to match personalities to illnesses was done by F. O. Ring in 1957.[4] Since then, numerous studies have been conducted in an effort to match attitudes, emotions, and behavior patterns with specific illnesses. Meyer Friedman and Ray Rosenman have conducted several recent studies of the relationship between a certain type of personality and heart attacks.[5] Other studies of the relationship between personality and disease have been done by Norman Greenfield and Richard A. Sternbach[6] and by Kenneth Pelletier.[7]

Personality needs to be considered as a contributory factor in the development of stress-related diseases. Pelletier has stated, "Evidence is accumulating that specific personality configurations may be associated with heart disease, cancer, and arthritis, as well as ulcerative colitis, asthma, migraine, and other disorders generally designated as psychosomatic or stress induced."

Human beings have the potential to live much longer than they usually do—at least 110 years.[8] Countless variables determine whether a person actually lives this long—one of which is the quality of that person's life. Research findings indicate that each individual has an organ or system that is most affected by constant and inappropriate elicitation of the stress response, and that there is a relationship between personality and vulnerable organ or system. That is why some of us develop cancer (immune system) while others develop coronary heart disease (cardiovascular system), for example. The notion that each of us has a particularly vulnerable organ or system is known as the "weak link theory."

This theory is based on the hypothesis that each organ, cell, and tissue has a finite amount of energy with which to adapt to the onslaught of stress, to the wear and tear of living. As this adaptation energy is depleted, the organ breaks down and wears out. In support of this theory, Selye has stated, "Among all my autopsies . . . I have never seen a person who died of old age. In fact, I do not think anyone has ever died of old age yet."[9] Selye claims that, for an individual to die of old age, all of the organs in that person's body would have to wear out simultaneously because they were simply used too long. But this is not what happens. A person dies when one vital part has worn out before the others. One vital link stops functioning, the finite amount of adaptation energy is exhausted, and the body as a whole can no longer survive. Selye concludes that "there is always one part which wears out first and wrecks the whole human machinery, merely because the other parts cannot function without it."[10]

## LIFE EVENTS, ACCIDENTS, AND DISEASE

Thomas Holmes developed an instrument—the Social Readjustment Rating Scale (SRRS)—for measuring psychosocial stressors and demonstrated how the accumulation of stressors in a short time can cause illness and accidents. Holmes and his associates listed forty-three life events that require adaptation or coping behavior by an individual.[11] It doesn't matter if the events are desirable or undesirable. Rather, it is the nature and frequency of these events that count.

Holmes assigned a magnitude score to each of the forty-three events. These scores, which range from 11 to 100 points, are called Life Change Units (LCUs). The event requiring the most coping and adaptation is the death of a spouse—100 points. The event requiring the least was a minor violation of the law—11 points.[12] This scale can be used to determine when an individual is accumulating a large number of points in a short period of time. Theoretically, the more life changes occurring, the greater the physiological changes and the greater the use of body energy to stave off the stressors. According to Holmes, it is possible to predict with some accuracy the onset of an illness or injury.

Holmes and his associates have studied various groups, from football players to pregnant women. They found that if a person had accumulated 300 or more points on the scale within the previous twelve months, that person had approximately an 80 percent chance of developing an illness, becoming severely depressed, or sustaining an injury within six months. If a person accumulates 150–299 points, the chance diminishes to 51 percent; with 150 points or less, an individual has a 37 percent chance of developing illness, injury, or depression.

Holmes suggests that when an individual must cope with many changes in a short time, the body remains in high gear. When he lets his guard down, illness and disease strike because body resistance has been lowered. At such times the body is particularly vulnerable to communicable diseases, such as common colds, flus, and other respiratory infections.

Let's look at the events during six months in the life of one man— Gary—to see how the Social Readjustment Rating Scale can be used to predict the onset of illness. As you read this story about Gary, refer to the scale (Table 3-1) and add up the points Gary accumulates.

Gary had been teaching elementary school while finishing work on his

TABLE 3-1
*The Social Readjustment Rating Scale*

| *Life Event* | *Mean Value* |
|---|---|
| 1. Death of spouse | 100 |
| 2. Divorce | 73 |
| 3. Marital separation | 65 |
| 4. Jail term | 63 |
| 5. Death of close family member | 63 |
| 6. Personal injury or illness | 53 |
| 7. Marriage | 50 |
| 8. Fired at work | 47 |
| 9. Marital reconciliation | 45 |
| 10. Retirement | 45 |
| 11. Change in health of family member | 44 |
| 12. Pregnancy | 40 |
| 13. Sexual difficulties | 39 |
| 14. Gain of new family member | 39 |
| 15. Business readjustment | 39 |
| 16. Change in financial state | 38 |
| 17. Death of close friend | 37 |
| 18. Change to different line of work | 36 |
| 19. Change in number of arguments with spouse | 35 |
| 20. Mortgage over $10,000 | 31 |
| 21. Foreclosure of mortgage or loan | 30 |
| 22. Change in responsibilities at work | 29 |
| 23. Son or daughter leaving home | 29 |
| 24. Trouble with in-laws | 29 |
| 25. Outstanding personal achievement | 28 |
| 26. Spouse begin or stop work | 26 |
| 27. Begin or end school | 26 |
| 28. Change in living conditions | 25 |
| 29. Revision of personal habits | 24 |
| 30. Trouble with boss | 23 |
| 31. Change in work hours or conditions | 20 |
| 32. Change in residence | 20 |
| 33. Change in schools | 20 |
| 34. Change in recreation | 19 |
| 35. Change in church activities | 19 |
| 36. Change in social activities | 18 |

TABLE 3-1

| Life Event | Mean Value |
|---|---|
| 37. Mortgage or loan less than $10,000 | 17 |
| 38. Change in sleeping habits | 16 |
| 39. Change in number of family get-togethers | 15 |
| 40. Change in eating habits | 15 |
| 41. Vacation | 13 |
| 42. Christmas | 12 |
| 43. Minor violations of the law | 11 |

Interpretation

Refer to the score range below to classify your life change score.

| Score Range | Interpretation | Susceptibility |
|---|---|---|
| 300+ | Major life change | Major illness within year |
| 250–299 | Serious life change | Lowered resistance to diseases |
| 200–249 | Moderate life change | Depression |
| 150–199 | Mild life change | Colds, flus, occasional depression |
| 149–0 | Very little life change | Good health |

General Observations

1. Change in one's life is followed, about a year later, by associated health changes. Is this true of your life style?
2. Life changes tend to cluster significantly around health changes. Is this true in your case?

SOURCE: T. H. Holmes and R. H. Rahe, "The Social Readjustment Rating Scale," *Journal of Psychosomatic Research* 11 (1967): 213–218. Copyright 1967, Pergamon Press, Ltd.

masters degree. In June he resigned from his job, even though he had not yet found another one. He was a little worried, but his wife was earning $15,000 a year, and Gary was pretty sure he would find a job teaching high school before the fall semester began.

During the eight-week summer session, Gary completed fifteen credit hours, including a research project, and at the end of the summer he received his masters degree. After graduation, Gary and his wife went to a party, and the next day they left for a short vacation. On the way up to the lake, Gary was stopped by the highway patrol for speeding and was given a ticket.

Gary and Gail had only been at the lake for three days when he got a call about a possible job. They interrupted their vacation and went home, so that Gary could make application and be interviewed. And within a few days Gary was offered the job, teaching high school in a city about a hundred miles from the town in which they had been living. Gary signed the contract, Gail resigned from her job, they bought a house near the new job, and moved. They were excited about starting a new life but also worried about having less income (about $10,000 less per year) and more financial responsibilities in the form of a large mortgage.

About a month later they took a weekend trip to see their old friends, and on the way back to the city they were involved in a head-on crash. Gail and Gary were both injured, and their car was totaled. Gary was unable to teach for several weeks. When he went back to work, he found that he had been assigned additional responsibilities.

It took Gary a while to adjust, and he encountered a number of setbacks and frustrations. But by Thanksgiving the job seemed to be going well, and Gary was able to slow down and relax for the first time in several months. Now, think about the many major life change events Gary had experienced during the six months described. What do you suppose happened during the four-day Thanksgiving vacation?

Gary developed a severe upper respiratory infection that lasted for the entire Thanksgiving vacation and hung on through the Christmas season as well. He was ill for almost seven weeks. Gary had accumulated more than 700 points during the previous eight months. Table 3-2 lists the major events in Gary's life during this period, and these add up to 414 points. But when points for other life events during the year of graduate work are added, the total goes over 700 points. For example, Gary commuted 400 miles round trip for seventeen weekends. His working conditions, living situation, sexual activities, and personal habits all changed.

Remember: An individual who accumulates 300 or more points has an 80 percent chance of illness. All of the life change events prior to the illness lead to the illness, and the illness adds points. Thus, it appears that illness

TABLE 3-2
*Gary's Accumulated Stress*

| Event | Points |
|---|---|
| Resigning job (retirement) | 39 |
| Change in financial state | 38 |
| Outstanding achievement (graduation) | 28 |
| Ceasing formal school | 26 |
| Vacation | 13 |
| Minor violation of the law | 11 |
| Change in line of work | 36 |
| Mortgage | 31 |
| Change in responsibilities of work | 29 |
| Spouse ceasing work | 26 |
| Change of residence | 20 |
| Change in working conditions | 20 |
| Illness | 53 |
| Change in health of family member | 44 |
| Total | 414 |

tends to beget illness. Accidents and injuries occur when point totals are high because the body is struggling to maintain balance and the mind is preoccupied with stressors.

Now think about your own life. When was the last time you were sick or had an injury? Examine the six months just prior to that time to see the number and kind of life-change events (stressors) you were experiencing. Total your points and see if there is a correlation between the accumulated changes and your illness or injury.

It is possible, of course, for a person with well over 300 points to remain well—that's the other 20 percent. Such people seem to have exceptionally high resistance, or they take things in stride. It is also possible for a person with fewer than 150 points to become ill. How each person handles stressors and how much each person can tolerate determines the effects of stressors.

Through the years, the SRRS has undergone a variety of changes and has been used with a variety of populations. Most of the scales have been directed toward the adult population. However, stress and adaptation are also part of the lives of children and college students, and so other life event inventories have been designed to predict onset of illness in these populations.[13]

TABLE 3-3
*LCU Scores for Each of Life-Change Events on CSRE*

| Column A | | Life-Change Event | Column B | Column C |
|---|---|---|---|---|
| _____ | (1) | Entered college | 50 | 50 |
| _____ | (2) | Married | 77 | _____ |
| _____ | (3) | Trouble with your boss | 38 | _____ |
| ___2___ | (4) | Held a job while attending school | 43 | 86 |
| _____ | (5) | Experienced the death of a spouse | 87 | _____ |
| _____ | (6) | Major change in sleeping habits | 34 | 34 |
| _____ | (7) | Experienced the death of a close family member | 77 | _____ |
| _____ | (8) | Major change in eating habits | 30 | 3? |
| _____ | (9) | Change in or choice of major field of study | 41 | _____ |
| _____ | (10) | Revision of personal habits | 45 | 45 |
| _____ | (11) | Experienced the death of a close friend | 68 | _____ |
| _____ | (12) | Found guilty of minor violations of the law | 22 | _____ |
| _____ | (13) | Had an outstanding personal achievement | 40 | _____ |
| _____ | (14) | Experienced pregnancy, or fathered a pregnancy | 68 | _____ |
| _____ | (15) | Major change in health or behavior of family member | 56 | 56 |
| _____ | (16) | Had sexual difficulties | 58 | 58 |
| _____ | (17) | Had trouble with in-laws | 42 | _____ |
| _____ | (18) | Major change in number of family get-togethers | 26 | _____ |
| _____ | (19) | Major change in financial state | 53 | 106 |
| _____ | (20) | Gained a new family member | 50 | _____ |
| _____ | (21) | Change in residence or living conditions | 42 | 84 |
| _____ | (22) | Major conflict or change in values | 50 | 50 |
| _____ | (23) | Major change in church activities | 36 | _____ |
| _____ | (24) | Marital reconciliation with your mate | 58 | _____ |
| _____ | (25) | Fired from work | 62 | _____ |
| _____ | (26) | Were divorced | 76 | _____ |
| _____ | (27) | Changed to a different line of work | 50 | 100 |
| _____ | (28) | Major change in number of arguments with spouse | 50 | _____ |

TABLE 3-3 continued

| Column A | Life-Change Event | Column B | Column C |
|---|---|---|---|
| _____(29) | Major change in responsibilities at work | 47 | 94 |
| _____(30) | Had your spouse begin or cease work outside the home | 41 | _____ |
| _____(31) | Major change in working hours or conditions | 42 | 42 |
| _____(32) | Marital separation from mate | 74 | _____ |
| _____(33) | Major change in type and/or amount of recreation | 37 | 37 |
| _____(34) | Major change in use of drugs | 52 | _____ |
| _____(35) | Took on a mortgage or loan of less than $10,000 | 52 | _____ |
| _____(36) | Major personal injury or illness | 65 | _____ |
| _____(37) | Major change in use of alcohol | 46 | _____ |
| _____(38) | Major change in social activities | 43 | _____ |
| _____(39) | Major change in amount of participation in school activities | 38 | _____ |
| _____(40) | Major change in amount of independence and responsibility | 49 | 97 |
| _____(41) | Took a trip or a vacation | 33 | 33 |
| _____(42) | Engaged to be married | 54 | _____ |
| _____(43) | Changed to a new school | 50 | 50 |
| _____(44) | Changed dating habits | 41 | 41 |
| _____(45) | Trouble with school administration | 44 | _____ |
| _____(46) | Broke or had broken a marital engagement or steady relationship | 60 | 60 |
| _____(47) | Major change in self-concept or self-awareness | 57 | 57 |
| | | TOTAL | _____ |

SOURCE: Martin B. Marx, Thomas F. Garrity, and Frank R. Bowers, "The Influence of Recent Life Experiences on the Health of College Freshmen," *Journal of Psychosomatic Research* 19 (1975): 97. Copyright 1975, Pergamon Press Ltd.

A version of the SRRS for college students was presented in a study by Martin Marx and his associates in 1974.[14] The authors listed forty-seven life change events that require the body to adapt. This study found that the link between major life changes and illnesses is also evident in the college population. The scale is included here for college-age readers who wish to examine the amount of change occurring in their lives. All you have to do is place the number of times you have experienced an event during the past twelve months in Column A of Table 3-3, multiply that number by the score in Column B, place that number in Column C, and, finally, total Column C. If your score is 1,435 LCUs, you fall into the "high" category for developing an illness. If your score is 347 LCUs or less, you fall into the "low" category for developing an illness. The "medium" score is around 890 LCUs. As with the Holmes scale, this represents only the likelihood of illness or accident. Thus, susceptibility is a factor based on a cluster of life events.

Note that all of these scales list both desirable and undesirable changes. The real benefit of the scales is to alert us to the pace of life, so that we can plan for or slow down the changes that may make us susceptible to health problems. Any life change has the potential to upset equilibrium and body balance. It is not one specific event that leads to illness—it is the body's effort to right itself, to restore homeostasis, that requires adaptation. It is this adaptation process and energy expenditure to restore homeostasis to which the general adaptation syndrome applies.

## THE GENERAL ADAPTATION SYNDROME

One interesting theory regarding stress and its effects on human systems has been suggested by Hans Selye. He identified three stages of the body's response to a life event or stressor. He called the three stages the General Adaptation Syndrome (GAS).[15] The three stages primarily encompass the endocrine physiology discussed earlier. These stages are (1) the alarm reaction, (2) resistance, and (3) exhaustion (see Figure 3-2).

According to Selye's theory, while the body is functioning within the normal level of resistance, it is able to function at an optimum level, which is a balanced state. The instant a stressor is registered and the endocrine physiology is activated, there is a slight dip below the normal level of resistance as the body prepares to cope. This is the alarm reaction—the body has awakened to the stressor.

After the initial reaction to the stressor, the body adapts or adjusts to that stressor in an effort to right itself. The adaptation occurs primarily because the nervous and endocrine systems help the body deal with the

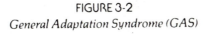

FIGURE 3-2
*General Adaptation Syndrome (GAS)*

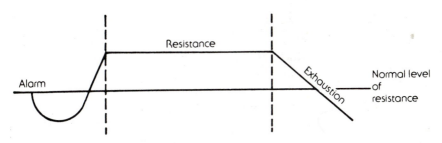

SOURCE: Figure 3 (p. 39) in *Stress Without Distress* by Hans
Selye (J. B. Lippincott Company). Copyright © 1974 by Hans
Selye, M.D. Reprinted by permission of Harper & Row, Pub-
lishers, Inc.

stressor. This has appropriately been labeled the stage of resistance. Generally, each of us goes through the first two stages regularly, with no significant
impact on well-being, because stressors are placed before us and removed
with regularity. The third stage—exhaustion—occurs when a stressor is not
removed or reinterpreted as a nonstressor.

The intensity of the stressor, the amount of time spent in resistance,
and the overall ability of a person to adjust to the stressor determine whether
the body energy falls below the normal level of resistance. This is the stage of
exhaustion, the point at which the body becomes most susceptible to disease and illness. If disruption of homeostasis continues, illness and death
could result.

Selye asserts that during this adaptation process, something in the
body gets used up. No one knows exactly what this "something" is or what it
does. Selye calls it "adaptation energy." It is hypothesized by Selye that each
person inherits just so much of it at birth. Because it is finite, exposure to
stressors determines how fast this adaptation energy gets used up. It is the
wear and tear of living and the use of this adaptation energy that leads to
what we call aging.

Many people believe that after they have exposed themselves to very
stressful activities, a rest can restore them to where they were
before. . . . Experiments on animals have clearly shown that each
exposure leaves an indelible scar in that it uses up reserves of adapt-
ability which cannot be replaced. It is true that immediately after
some harassing experience, rest can restore us almost to the original
level of fitness by eliminating acute fatigue. But the emphasis is on

the word almost. Since we constantly go through periods of stress and rest during life, even a minute deficit of adaptation energy every day adds up—it adds up to what we call aging.[16]

Many writers, including Selye, relate life style and the use of adaptation energy to the aging process. Selye states that "aging results from the sum of all the stressors to which the body has been exposed during a lifetime."[17] As we progress through life experiences, the GAS is called into action many times. During each of the three stages, adaptation energy is used (see Figure 3-3). The greatest amount of energy is used during the third stage. It is in this stage that the greatest demands are placed upon the body. It is also a prime time for primary-secondary stressor cycles to develop, and these place constant stress on the body. The body under stress never fully returns to the original level of balance, because the finite pool of adaptive energy slowly becomes depleted. Let's examine Figure 3-3 further.

Notice that the first alarm reaction and use of adaptation occurs at birth. We know that the infant experiences a great deal of trauma at birth and that a tremendous adjustment must be made for survival outside of the womb. From that moment on, life is a series of adjustments—of stress responses and utilization of adaptation energy. Eventually, some stressor or a cycle of primary-secondary stressors depletes the pool of adaptation energy. Exhaustion becomes total, and death occurs.

FIGURE 3-3
*Utilization of Adaptive Energy*

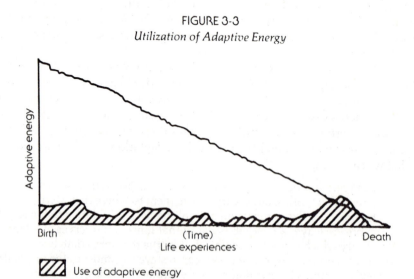

Birth     (Time)                    Death
Life experiences

Use of adaptive energy

An individual's life style and ability to adjust or cope with stressors seems partly to determine the rate of utilization of adaptive energy. The theory implies that if a person can minimize the amount of time spent in the resistance stage and especially in the exhaustion stage, the person can slow the use of nonreplaceable adaptation energy. If a person regularly overreacts or acts inappropriately to stressors, depletion of adaptation energy is speeded up. Physical fitness and stress management programs that help offset some of the physiological changes produced by the stress response can slow the depletion of adaptation energy.

It should be noted here that this is only a theory and has not been validated through research. However, the logic of this theory makes sense, and it should be considered if we are interested in getting our lives under control and preventing stress gone bad.

## SUMMARY

Each person seems to have a baseline of tolerable stress. As long as we remain within these limits, there is little impairment to health. When body rhythm is broken—either by too many stressors in a short period of time or by a barrage of stressors over a long period of time—the stress response is elicited too frequently and opens the door for potential problems. Neither fighting nor fleeing is an appropriate response to most modern stressors, which are not life threatening but do occur frequently.

Often the result of inappropriate and constant elicitation of the stress response is, first, a slight alteration of the autonomic and endocrine functioning. Without intervention, this is likely to be followed by a more dramatic change. It is at this point that we see "stress gone bad" in the form of stress-related illnesses. Individual personality and genetic makeup appear to play a role in determining which diseases and specific body organs and systems are affected.

Several tools have been developed to assist individuals in determining how many stressful life events are occurring and what behavior adjustment is needed. The Holmes and Rahe Social Readjustment Rating Scale is one tool for measuring change, desirable or undesirable, and predicting the onset of illness and accidents. This scale has been used in research and adapted to various special populations, including college students. The scale can be used to assess the number of life events we are encountering, so that we can plan the pace at which future events are encountered.

Many authors and researchers have attempted to explain how elicitation of the stress response is related to the aging process. Selye's General

Adaptation Syndrome is based on the idea that when a stressor is perceived, the body reacts in three stages: the alarm stage, the resistance stage, and the exhaustion stage. The intensity of the stressor and the length of time spent in each stage determine how much "adaptation energy" (a term coined by Selye) is used. The pool of adaptation energy is finite. The accumulation of stressors throughout a person's life eventually depletes this pool, and death occurs. Selye's theory implies that how we live, how we perceive stressors, and how we react to stressors make a difference in the amount of distress—of "stress gone bad"—we experience.

### Notes

1  Alvin Toffler, *Future Shock* (New York: Random House, 1970), p. 13.

2  Adrian M. Osterfeld and Richard Shekelle, in *Relax: How You Can Feel Better, Reduce Stress, and Overcome Tension*, eds. John White and James Fadiman (The Confucian Press, 1976), pp. 48–49.

3  Kenneth R. Pelletier, *Mind as Healer, Mind as Slayer: A Holistic Approach to Preventing Stress Disorders* (New York: Dell, 1977), p. 117.

4  F. O. Ring, "Testing the Validity of Personality Profiles in Psychosomatic Illnesses," *American Journal of Psychiatry* 113 (1957): 1075–1080.

5  Meyer Friedman and Ray H. Rosenman, "Association of Specific Overt Behavior Pattern with Blood and Cardiovascular Findings," *Journal of the American Medical Association* 169 (1959): 1286–1296; Meyer Friedman and Ray H. Rosenman, *Type A Behavior and Your Heart* (New York: Knopf, 1974); Ray H. Rosenman, Meyer Friedman, C. D. Jenkins, R. Straus, M. Wurm, and R. Kostichek, "Clinically Unrecognized Myocardial Infarction in the Western Collaborative Group Study," *American Journal of Cardiology* 19 (1967): 776–782; Ray H. Rosenman, Meyer Friedman, R. Straus, M. Wurm, H. Messinger, and C. D. Jenkins, "Coronary Heart Disease in the Western Collaborative Group Study: A Follow-up Experiment of Two Years," *Journal of the American Medical Association* 195 (1966): 86–92.

6  Norman Greenfield and Richard A. Sternbach, eds., *Handbook of Psychophysiology* (New York: Holt, Rinehart, and Winston, 1972), pp. 839–917.

7  Pelletier, *Mind as Healer, Mind as Slayer*, p. 119.

8  Leonard Hayflick, as cited in "Can Aging Be Cured?" *Newsweek* April 16, 1973, p. 63.

9  Hans Selye, *The Stress of Life* (New York: McGraw-Hill, 1976), p. 431.

10  Ibid., p. 432.

11  Thomas H. Holmes and Richard H. Rahe, "The Social Readjustment Rating Scale," *Journal of Psychosomatic Research* 11 (1967): 213.

12  M. Masuda and T. H. Holmes, "Magnitude Estimation of Social Readjustments," *Journal of Psychosomatic Research* 11 (1967): 219.

13  R. D. Coddington, "The Significance of Life Events as Etiologic Factors in the Disease of Children," *Journal of Psychosomatic Research* 16 (1972): 205–214.

14  Martin B. Marx, Thomas F. Garrity, and Frank R. Bowers, "The Influence of Recent Life Experiences on the Health of College Freshmen," *Journal of Psychosomatic Research* 19 (1975): 87–98.

15 Hans Selye, *Stress Without Distress* (New York: New American Library, 1974), p. 27.

16 Ibid., p. 93.

17 Hans Selye, *The Stress of Life*, p. 429.

## References

Coddington, R. D. "The Significance of Life as Etiologic Factors in the Disease of Children." *Journal of Psychosomatic Research* 16 (1972): 205–214.

Friedman, Meyer, and Rosenman, Ray H. "Association of Specific Overt Behavior Pattern with Blood and Cardiovascular Findings." *Journal of the American Medical Association* 169 (1959): 1286–1296.

Friedman, Meyer, and Rosenman, Ray H. *Type A Behavior and Your Heart.* New York: Alfred A. Knopf, 1974.

Holmes, Thomas H., and Rahe, Richard A. "The Social Readjustment Rating Scale." *Journal of Psychosomatic Research,* 1967.

Marx, Martin B; Garrity, Thomas F.; and Bowers, Frank R. "The Influence of Recent Life Experiences on the Health of College Freshmen." *Journal of Psychosomatic Research* 19 (1975): 87–98.

Masuda, M., and Holmes, Thomas H. "Magnitude Estimation of Social Readjustments." *Journal of Psychosomatic Research* 11 (1967): 219.

Osterfeld, Adrian M., and Shekelle, Richard. As cited in White, John, and Fadiman, James, eds. *Relax: How You Can Feel Better, Reduce Stress, and Overcome Tension.* New York: Confucian Press, 1976.

Pelletier, Kenneth R. *Mind as Healer, Mind as Slayer: A Holistic Approach to Preventing Stress Disorders.* New York: Dell, 1977.

Ring, F. O. "Testing the Validity of Personality Profiles in Psychosomatic Illnesses." *American Journal of Psychiatry* 113 (1957): 1075–1080.

Rosenman, Ray H.; Friedman, Meyer; Jenkins, C. D.; Straus, R.; Wurm, M.; and Kostichek, R. "Clinically Unrecognized Myocardial Infarction in the Western Collaborative Group Study." *American Journal of Cardiology* 19 (1967): 776–782.

Rosenman, Ray H.; Friedman, Meyer; Straus, R.; Wurm, R.; Messinger, H.; and Jenkins, C. D. "Coronary Heart Disease in the Western Collaborative Group Study: A Follow-Up Experiment of Two Years." *Journal of the American Medical Association* 195 (1966): 86–92.

Selye, Hans. *Stress Without Distress.* New York: New American Library, 1974.

Selye, Hans. *The Stress of Life.* New York: McGraw-Hill, 1976.

Toffler, Alvin. *Future Shock.* New York: Random House, 1970.

# BENEFITS OF
# RELAXATION

"Slow down." "Take it easy." "Relax." Years ago these words were very much a part of Granny's recipe for moderate and healthful living. Today, physicians and allied health professionals give this advice to overstressed patients and to the population at large. We each need to maintain balance within ourselves and in relationship to the environment. Maintaining this balance is not easy today.

Many people don't know how to relax; many don't perceive the need to relax; and most say they don't have time to relax. We have found that people who don't have time to relax are probably the ones who need to the most. In chapters 5 through 12, we will talk about how to relax. We must each decide for ourselves whether we need to relax. In this chapter, we discuss what relaxation is and what it is not, and we talk about the benefits of practicing relaxation skills regularly.

The benefits described here in general terms have been confirmed by research. To find out more about the research, we suggest reading some of the sources listed at the end of the chapter.

## RELAXATION: WHAT IT IS AND WHAT IT IS NOT

Watching television may be a stress reducer, but it is not relaxation. The same is true of hiking, gardening, reading, playing cards, hunting, fishing, or basket weaving. These may be constructive uses of leisure time. And it may be true that these activities intervene in the stress cycle. They may help us to slow down, to take it easy, to keep our work in proper perspective, along with the rest of our lives. These activities divert attention from stressors or potential stressors and help maintain balance or even restore homeostasis. There is much value in diversion, and we don't want to deny such activities or their benefits. But these are not forms of relaxation.

Relaxation is a physiological state that is the opposite of the stress state. It involves skills that elicit the physiological response that is the opposite of the fight-or-flight response. In speaking about this opposite response, Herbert Benson has written:

> Each of us possesses a natural and innate protective mechanism against "overstress," which allows us to turn off harmful bodily effects, to counter the effects of the fight-or-flight response. This response against "overstress" brings on bodily changes that decrease heart rate, lower metabolism, decrease the rate of breathing, and bring the body back into what is probably a healthier balance.[1]

To elicit this relaxation response we can use a number of practical tools called *relaxation exercises*. We can thus learn how to elicit the natural and innate response we call relaxation. Use of these specific exercises to elicit the relaxation response yields observable and measurable results. The most beneficial relaxation techniques are those that are most effective in counteracting stress and offsetting the negative aspects of the stress response.

## INTERVENING IN THE STRESS CYCLE

The diagram in Figure 4-1 summarizes the stress cycle. The ideal point to intervene in this cycle is Point A. Intervention at this point is prophylactic and/or nourishing.

There is evidence that people who practice relaxation skills regularly (in particular, forms of meditation) are likely to be more psychologically and physiologically stable, less anxious, and in greater control of their lives than people who do not.[2] Perhaps the quieting effect relaxation has on the cerebral cortex helps the individual to perceive stressors as less threatening and so to avoid overreaction. There is then a lower emotional arousal, which seems to explain why some individuals do not overreact to stressors. Reaction for adaptation and adjustment occurs, but overreaction that intensifies the stress response may diminish. Should stressors be encountered and the stress response elicited, there is a quicker return to homeostasis. A person who can elicit a state almost totally opposite to the stress response is free not to

FIGURE 4-1
*Points of Intervention in the Stress Cycle*

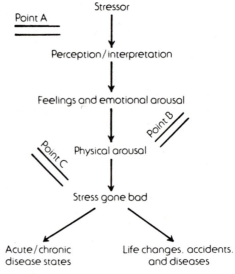

A = Personality engineering
B = Relaxation training
C = Exercise and medical care

Adapted from Daniel Girdano and George Everly, *Controlling Stress and Tension: A Holistic Approach* (Englewood Cliffs, N. J.: 1979), pp. 22–26.

overreact to the stressors and, if reaction does occur, to achieve a faster return to balance.[3]

Thus, relaxation exercises used at Point A extend the individual's ability to tolerate stress. People who practice relaxation exercises approach life events in a more relaxed manner, don't overreact as often, and return to balance more rapidly. Relaxation keeps the autonomic nervous and endocrine systems functioning within reasonable limits.

Intervention at Point A should also include what Daniel A. Girdano and George S. Everly call personality engineering and social engineering. They describe social engineering as "the willful altering of life style and/or general environment in order to modify exposure to needless stressors."[4] These researchers suggest personality—which they say is composed of values, attitudes, and behavior patterns—determines how an individual defines or interprets a life event. Alteration of one of these components (values, attitudes, or behavior) is a step toward reducing stress. The intentional alteration of the stressful aspects of personality is called "personality engineering."[5] Any educational program, any increase of self-awareness, any self-assessment in which we try to make sense out of our reactions to stressors and assign meaning to them, is beneficial as a first step in a stress management program.

The strategies of communication and time management described in Chapters 14 and 15 are useful at this point. Point A is a good time for self-examination, for examination of purpose and direction in life. This value clarification process can help the individual improve self-concept and move toward self-actualization. The Holmes and Rahe Social Readjustment Rating Scale is useful for assessing the pace and numbers of life events being experienced. If we are aware that stress is affecting our bodys' senses, we can then devise appropriate nourishment. Assessment facilitates beneficial intervention and nourishment, reinforcement, and motivation for more effective involvement with our lives.

## LIFE STYLE

Each individual develops a life style—a way of living—that is determined by his or her values, attitudes, interests, beliefs, and circumstances. Relaxation exercises can help to modify the impact of some stressors within a particular life style. Research in the area of life style changes is inconclusive because of the difficulty in establishing direct cause–effect relationships between the use of relaxation techniques and changes in life style. There are too many variables that cannot be controlled in research studies. However, many people who practice some form of relaxation exercise regularly have reported changes in their use of chemical substances. These include reduction or elimination of alcohol intake, cigarette smoking, and coffee consumption. Changes in diet, sleeping patterns, and coping ability have also been reported.[6] Alcohol, nicotine, inadequate nutrition, and insomnia are all potential stressors that can influence the quality of a person's life style.

Founded more in wisdom and observation than research are the ideas of Don Ardell, author of *High-Level Wellness: An Alternative to Doctors, Drugs, and Disease.* Ardell says that the more positive things we do for ourselves, the fewer negative things we do against ourselves. The use of exercises to elicit the relaxation response is one of the positive things we can do for our bodies and minds, especially at Point A in the stress cycle. As positive changes occur, we feel better about ourselves, and we gain some confidence in our abilities to control and direct the forces affecting our lives.

This serves as reinforcement and as motivation to continue using relaxation exercises, along with other strategies to continue growing, and to continue doing more positive things for ourselves and fewer negative things against ourselves.

Relaxation exercises evoke innate and integrated physiological changes that are almost the opposite of the fight-or-flight (stress) response. These physiological changes have been dubbed the "relaxation response" by Herbert Benson. The relaxation techniques that elicit this response and are most useful at Point B are (1) meditation, (2) Benson's method, (3) standard autogenic training, (4) hypnosis with suggested relaxation, (5) biofeedback training, and (6) progressive muscle relaxation. Use of these methods brings about an overall decrease in body metabolism that results in a decreased heart and breathing rate, decreased oxygen utilization within the body, decreased blood pressure, and decreased muscular tension in major muscle groups. And so these methods are particularly useful in restoring body balance after physical arousal. If practiced regularly, they are also useful prior to physical arousal. Then, when the stress response is elicited, it may not be as intense, and return to a balanced state will be faster. A comparison of various relaxation exercises and accompanying physical changes is presented in Table 4-1. This table reports only responses that have been scientifically measured.

Many of us lead hectic lives and have overcrowded schedules, and we are still tense when it is time to go to sleep. Our bodies are fatigued and need rest. But how often have you gotten into bed, turned out the light, closed your eyes—and found many of the day's events or upcoming events racing through your mind? As stressful events are relived in the mind, the body continues to respond (physical arousal) as it did in the original encounter. Relaxation skills, especially progressive relaxation techniques, have been found to be useful in reducing the time between entering the sleep situation and the reported onset of sleep, and also in the treatment of insomnia.[7] Quieting the muscles reduces neural impulses to and from the brain, and that results in a relaxed condition in which both body and mind are ready for sleep. (See chapter 12, for more information on sleep and sleep techniques.)

Prolonged and constant elicitation of the stress response can alter the neurophysiology of the body, eventually leading to many of the stress-induced diseases or illnesses. Because of the specific and combined physiological benefits of the relaxation response, relaxation exercises are useful in the stress-gone-bad cycle, Point C in Figure 4-1. Generally, at this point a doctor is consulted, and some form of treatment is prescribed. Relaxation exercises used at this point are most effective in conjunction with a treatment program prescribed by a physician or health-care provider. A partnership between the

TABLE 4-1
Comparison of Methods for Eliciting Total Body Relaxation

| | Oxygen Consumption | Respiratory Rate | Heart Rate | Blood Pressure | Muscular Tension |
|---|---|---|---|---|---|
| Progressive relaxation | Not measured | Not measured | Not measured | Inconclusive | Decreases |
| Benson's method | Decreases | Decreases | Decreases | Decreases | Not measured |
| Transcendental meditation | Decreases | Decreases | Decreases | Decreases[a] | Not measured |
| Zen and yoga | Decreases | Decreases | Decreases | Decreases[a] | Not measured |
| Hypnosis with suggested relaxation | Decreases | Decreases | Decreases | Inconclusive | Not measured |

[a]In patients with elevated blood pressure

Adapted from: Herbert Benson, with Miriam Z. Klipper, *The Relaxation Response* (New York: William Morrow, 1975), and John White and James Fadiman, *Relax: How You Can Feel Better, Reduce Stress, and Overcome Tension* (Confucian Press, 1976), p. 52.

medical profession and those who teach relaxation techniques should be encouraged. Both approaches are necessary and beneficial for a holistic approach to stress management.

Is it possible to retrain the nervous and endocrine systems with relaxation exercises? Research findings suggest that it is possible to alter, in a positive manner, the neurophysiology of the body, so that it returns to a more balanced state. Benson and his associates have demonstrated how relaxation can lower high blood pressure.[8] Jacobson has reported on the effectiveness of progressive relaxation exercises in reducing the severity of spastic esophagus and colitis.[9] R. Honsberger and A. F. Wilson have demonstrated the effectiveness of relaxation skills (meditation) in improving airway resistance in improving bronchial asthma,[10] and Schwartz has demonstrated how relaxation skills can reduce tension headaches.[11] These benefits, plus others, result from allowing the neurophysiological pathways to return to a more balanced condition, so that they function at a more optimal level.

Following physical arousal, or even when stress has become distress, relaxation exercises alone may not be all that is needed. Once the stress response is elicited, adrenalin, noradrenalin, and free fatty acids are in general circulation. Strenuous physical exercise or recreational activity can help to utilize—to "burn up"—these substances. Diet, nutrition, and weight control may be necessary components of treatment. Medication also may be necessary, but it is important to remember that in the long run drugs can lead to their own set of problems. They may help in stabilizing physiology, but they offer little help in changing the source of stress and do not usually help an individual take responsibility for making changes that would reduce stress.

## COMBINED BENEFITS

In 1977 Ruanne Peters, Herbert Benson, and Douglas Porter conducted a study to assess the effectiveness of daily relaxation breaks on five self-reported measures of health, performance, and well-being.[12] Since the use of relaxation techniques appears to have a wide range of physiological and psychological effects, these researchers were interested not only in the physiological and psychological effects of relaxation in the working population but also in the interrelationships among these effects.

For the study, subjects (all employees of a company) were randomly divided into three groups. Group A were taught a specific technique (called *Benson's method*) for eliciting the relaxation response. Group B were instructed to take a relaxation break but asked not to use any special technique to help them during the break (they were untrained in the use of relaxation skills). Group C received no instructions about what to do during their breaks. Members of Group A and B were asked to take two 15-minute relaxation breaks each day for eight weeks. One break was to be taken in the morning and one in the afternoon. These researchers found:

1. Between the first and last sessions, the greatest decrease in symptoms was in Group A. (The symptoms index included thirty items that were predominantly physical, such as headache, nausea, rash, diarrhea, and mouth sores. In addition there were twenty-one items that were behavioral, such as difficulty in getting to sleep, worrying over trifles, recurring thoughts or dreams, and nervous habits like biting fingernails or chewing pencils.)

2. Groups A and B showed the greatest improvements. The amount of improvement decreased with Group A improving the most and Group C the least, on each of the following:
   a. illness index—used to note feelings of illness, fever, or pain at any time of the day;

b. performance index—used to rate perceived levels of physical energy, strength of concentration, handling of problems, and overall efficiency;

c. sociability-satisfaction index—used to assess how well things were going at home, with friends, roommates, people at work, and confidence in self.

These findings indicate that the practice of relaxation techniques is associated with greater improvements in self than is achieved by just sitting quietly. This study suggests that relaxation techniques could be used at both Points A and B and that they may change the individual's perceptions of stressors. It is difficult to categorize the benefits into specific areas, such as physical, psychological, and social, because benefits may overlap. Human beings bring all five dimensions into each of their life experiences, and all dimensions are affected. Relaxation exercises benefit the mind and the body—the whole person.

## SUMMARY

One way to intervene in the stress cycle is to select and practice relaxation techniques. Relaxation and diversion are not the same. Relaxation techniques are a systematic means of inducing a physiological response that is the opposite of the stress response. Diversions are activities that move attention away from stressors but do not necessarily induce a decrease in metabolism, heart and breathing rates, muscular tension, and other physiological changes that occur during relaxation.

Relaxation techniques have been found to be beneficial as an intervention strategy in the stress cycle and in altering some aspects of life style. Benefits include, but are not limited to: (1) being less anxious and so approaching life in a more relaxed manner; (2) learning to view stress and stressors in perspective; (3) reducing the use of biochemical stressors, such as tobacco and alcohol; (4) improving sleep onset; and (5) retraining the nervous and endocrine systems to reduce high blood pressure, spastic colitis, bronchial asthma, tension headaches, and other stress-related anomalies. Benefits are generally associated with the motivation and purpose a person takes into the relaxation exercise. Individuals may also perform relaxation exercises as a positive health practice simply to feel better and add a fresh perspective to daily routines. Regardless of purpose, relaxation exercises provide an opportunity for people to exercise greater control over the forces that affect life, health, and well-being.

## Notes

1 Herbert Benson, *The Relaxation Response* (New York: Avon, 1975), pp. 25–26.

2 Kenneth Pelletier, *Mind as Healer, Mind as Slayer: A Holistic Approach to Preventing Stress Disorders* (New York: Dell, 1977), p. 200.

3 Ibid., pp. 200–208.

4 Dan A. Girdano and George S. Everly, *Controlling Stress and Tension: A Holistic Approach* (Englewood Cliffs, N. J.: Prentice-Hall, 1979), p. 125.

5 Ibid., p. 144.

6 Pelletier, *Mind as Healer, Mind as Slayer*, p. 208.

7 Douglas A. Bernstein and Thomas D. Borkovec, *Progressive Relaxation Training: A Manual for the Helping Professions* (Champaign: Research Press, 1973), pp. 8–9; Pelletier, *Mind as Healer, Mind as Slayer*, p. 208.

8 Herbert Benson, B. A. Rosner, B. R. Marzetta, et. al., "Decreased Blood Pressure in Pharmacologically Treated Hypertensive Patients Who Regularly Elicited the Relaxation Response," *Lancet* 1 (1974): 289–291; Herbert Benson, B. A. Rosner, B. R. Marzetta, et. al., "Decreased Blood Pressure in Borderline Hypertensive Subjects Who Practiced Meditation," *Journal of Chronic Diseases* 27 (1974): pp. 163–169.

9 Edmund Jacobson, *You Must Relax* (New York: McGraw-Hill, 1976), pp. 75, 81.

10 R. Honsberger and A. F. Wilson, "Transcendental Meditation in Treating Asthma," *Respiratory Therapy: The Journal of Inhalation Technology* 3 (1973): 79–81.

11 Pelletier, *Mind as Healer, Mind as Slayer*, pp. 208–210.

12 Ruanne K. Peters, Herbert Benson, and Douglas Porter, "Daily Relaxation Response Breaks in a Working Population: I. Effects on Self-Reported Measures of Health, Performance, and Well-Being," *American Journal of Public Health* 67 (1977): pp. 946–953.

## References

Benson, Herbert. *The Relaxation Response*. New York: William Morrow, 1975.

Benson, Herbert; Rosner, B. A.; Marzetta, B. R., et. al. "Decreased Blood Pressure in Pharmacologically Treated Hypertensive Patients Who Regularly Elicited the Relaxation Response." *Lancet* 1 (1974): 289–291.

Benson, Herbert; Rosner, B. A.; Marzetta, B. R.; et. al. "Decreased Blood Pressure in Borderline Hypertensive Subjects Who Practiced Meditation." *Journal of Chronic Diseases* 27 (1974): 163–169.

Bernstein, Douglas A., and Borkovec, Thomas D. *Progressive Relaxation Training: A Manual for the Helping Professions*. Champaign: Research Press, 1973.

Girdano, Daniel A., and Everly, George S. *Controlling Stress and Tension: A Holistic Approach*. Englewood Cliffs, N. J.: Prentice-Hall, 1979.

Jacobson, Edmund. *You Must Relax*. New York: McGraw-Hill, 1976.

McQuade, Walter, and Aikman, Ann. *Stress: What It Is, What It Can Do To Your Health, How To Fight Back*. New York: Bantam, 1974.

Pelletier, Kenneth R. *Mind as Healer, Mind as Slayer: A Holistic Approach to Preventing Stress Disorders*. New York: Dell, 1977.

Peters, Ruanne K.; Benson, Herbert; and Porter, Douglas. "Daily Relaxation Response Breaks in a Working Population: I. Effects on Self-Reported Measures of Health, Performance, and Well-Being." *American Journal of Public Health* 67 (1977): 946–953.

Snider, A. "Young Asthma Victims Given No-Drug Therapy." *Science Digest* 73 (1973): 43–46.

# PART TWO

# FOUNDATIONS OF A RELAXATION PROGRAM

Now that we understand stress and the intent of a stress management program, let's look at exercises that can be used in a stress management program. The progression of exercises presented here has been developed over eight years; the use of this sequence facilitates the learning of these exercises.

In this part, the underlying philosophy for a relaxation program is discussed, and basic relaxation positions are identified. The chapters on sensory awareness, the breathing rhythms, and the supporting environment provide elementary techniques that aid relaxation. Practice Schedule Charts are provided for each exercise. Regular practice of the exercises suggested here is good preparation for the more advanced skills presented in Part Three.

# 5

███████████████

# THE BASIC
# ELEMENTS OF
# RELAXATION

This chapter provides basic information about the holistic approach to relaxation: the general philosophy of the relaxation program, important points to consider in advancing through the program, the basic elements required to achieve total relaxation, and the basic positions and variations of these positions in which to practice the skills.

## A HOLISTIC APPROACH

The holistic approach to a relaxation program presented here closely reflects the belief that stress is a normal, desirable part of life, that stress adds spice to our lives. Without stress our lives would be boring. Stress not only makes life worth living but is often the catalyst that propels us toward better performance, greater creativity, increased participation, adjustment to all types of demands, and increased enjoyment of life.

However, when stress begins to dominate our lives and erode enjoyment, when it contributes to greater susceptibility to illness, it is necessary to reexamine our life styles. Health requires that we control stress in our lives, so that it does not dominate us. If we find that stress is endangering our health, we need to begin to manage the stress and attempt to regain the control that has been eroded.

If we are to regain control, we must make a commitment to health as a major priority in our lives. When health is not a major priority, we are likely to plan our daily activities by scheduling other commitments and then trying to find the time needed to practice and live healthful behaviors. All too often this becomes self-defeating, because there is never time at the end of the day to meet health-related goals.

A commitment to a healthful life style involves reversing this process. We must establish time periods in which to practice healthful habits (relaxation exercises) and then schedule other commitments around those periods. For example, suppose that you have decided to begin a regular jogging and relaxation program. First, schedule a block of time for jogging and relaxation—say between noon and one o'clock. An hour gives you ample time to change, jog, shower, dress, and relax for ten minutes. Once this time is established, a true commitment means that you will not normally schedule anything else during this time. It also means that you will assume the responsibility to follow through on this commitment.

Each of us must accept responsibility for our own health. The major contemporary health problems—obesity, smoking, alcoholism, and stress—are related to behaviors that are usually self-chosen, behaviors we can change. The individual who makes a commitment to a healthful life style must take responsibility for choosing ways to fulfill that commitment. For example, it is essential to choose enhanced health and prevention of illnesses over cure. Cure is an after-the-fact behavior that perpetuates the attitude of "you take care of me." The individual is also responsible for establishing and maintaining healthful habits. Only you can select and follow the habits that will foster your health; you are responsible for the choices and changes you make.

Also, it is possible for us to change our personalities and philosophies of living, if we decide that that is what we want to do. The holistic relaxation program is not designed to change personality; a person who is competitive, aggressive, and hard driving will not likely select a slower approach to life  because of a relaxation program. The emphasis of the relaxation program is, rather, on regular, daily periods of relaxation that give the body time to relax physiologically and psychologically so it can have time to function in its homeostatic state, where all systems function best. Also, each person should recognize and assess his or her behavioral traits and know the consequences of these traits. Then that person can decide what behavior changes are desirable. Even if a person makes no personality changes, however, regular relaxation can help offset the consequences of stressful behavior.

## IMPORTANT BEGINNING POINTS
## FOR A HOLISTIC RELAXATION PROGRAM

Before you begin the relaxation program described in the following pages, consider the eight points below. This list is not intended to be all inclusive— an all-inclusive list would be endless.

1. This holistic relaxation program has been designed for healthy individuals without severe physical or psychological problems. If you have a physical or psychological problem, check with your personal physician before starting the relaxation exercises. This is absolutely necessary if you are under medication or medical supervision. This program is effective for individuals with poor health, if it is undertaken with the knowledge and supervision of a physician.

2. You are in control. You are not being forced to do any of the exercises, nor must you continue any of the exercises if you do not wish to. The exercise sequence and practice schedule should be undertaken with the understanding that each individual is unique. Each person has to eliminate, adapt, and even change the exercises and other recommendations to fit individual needs.

3. Some of the exercises will work for you, and others will not. Some exercises will work for the majority of the people who try them, practice them, and follow the recommended sequence. Some exercises may not work for you the first few times you try them, but relaxation is a skill, much like tennis and golf, and must be practiced until proficiency is achieved. Try the exercises with a passive attitude. Practice them, and when your body is ready—they will work. Practice makes perfect—but practice of relaxation skills cannot be forced.

Some of the exercises may cause stress, fear, or anxiety for some individuals. If this happens to you, stop that exercise and substitute a different exercise. Remember: You are in control, and you must assume responsibility for adjusting or adapting each exercise. It is even possible that you may try the exercises for a time, discover they do not work for you, and decide to stop the program.

4. The time of the day may be important for you. What is the best time of day for you to practice relaxation? Some individuals find that the early morning hours are best, while others find the evening hours, the noon hour, coffee breaks, or the time immediately after physical activity most beneficial. Some individuals use the relaxation exercises to help them to fall asleep. Others find that if they use relaxation exercises late in the evening they feel invigorated and unable to fall asleep afterward. Try the exercises at various

times of the day, to see when they best fit into your schedule, moods, and needs. When you are learning the exercises, practice them when you can relax under ideal circumstances. After the exercises have been learned, they can usually be done when you are under stress.

5. You may fall asleep when first learning the exercises. If this happens, adjust accordingly. If you have scheduled an appointment for after your relaxation practice, it may be wise to set an alarm clock. If you do use an alarm, muffle the alarm or keep it at a distance so that the sudden noise will not jolt you.

6. If you wear contact lenses, remove them during the exercises. Each individual is different, however, and you are the best judge of whether you can perform the exercises while wearing your contact lenses.

7. You should understand physiological changes that occur during relaxation. Although a variety of physiological changes take place during a state of deep relaxation, changes in heart and breathing rates are most noticeable. It is important to understand that these changes are common for healthy individuals and should not be of concern unless your physician indicates otherwise.

Most of the exercises require that you breathe normally. Do not force or try to control your breathing rhythm. This interferes with the relaxation process. Let your body determine your breathing rate. You may notice a change in the breathing rhythm as it slows down. This is normal during relaxation, because less oxygen is required as muscular tension diminishes.

As your sensory awareness increases, you may discover that you can tune into your heart beat. During relaxation the heart rate is likely to slow down suddenly. This is a normal response similar to the sudden change in the breathing rate. There is no need for concern—the body is adjusting to the decreased need for oxygen that results from reduced muscular tension. Usually decreased heart and breathing rates indicate that a more relaxed state has been achieved. Individuals who are concerned about heart rate (for example, cardiac patients) may want to discuss heart rate with their physicians. A doctor can explain to you the physiological changes that occur during relaxation. This knowledge can help you to be more comfortable with the exercises.

8. Record the exercises in the Practice Schedule Charts at the end of each chapter. One of the most important factors in changing behavior is awareness of the behavior to be changed. The Practice Schedule Charts are designed to keep you aware of the relaxation exercises to be performed. When used regularly, the charts will help you to incorporate relaxation into your daily schedule.

## LEARNING THE EXERCISES

A few basic guidelines facilitate the learning of sensory awareness and total body relaxation. If you follow these simple but important guidelines, your chances of success will be improved.

### A Quiet Environment

When learning the exercises, it is important to practice them in a quiet environment where there are few distractions. If possible, eliminate background noises and interruptions during practice sessions. This will allow you to concentrate on the exercises. After you have learned the exercises and are able to elicit the relaxed state, you will probably be able to practice the exercises in any environment where you feel comfortable. Many of the exercises presented in later chapters can be done in a noisy environment and in an active position. But when you are beginning to learn the exercises, you need to withdraw from your surroundings and from all external stimuli. Make yourself comfortable, close your eyes, and concentrate on the relaxation experience.

### A Comfortable Position

Most of the skills are best learned in a comfortable position in which the major muscle groups of the body are totally supported. Because position and support are vital to relaxation, this component is examined in detail in the next section.

### Concentration on Selected Exercise

Select an exercise. Study the exercise description until you know and understand the proper sequence for performing it. Often your mind will wander while you are performing an exercise. When you realize this has happened, focus on the exercise again. Either begin the exercise again or continue from where you were when your mind began to wander. Determine which is best by observing the level of relaxation you find yourself in when you realize your attention has shifted.

### A Passive Attitude

Do not force the skills. A passive attitude requires acceptance of what the body and mind dictate. Do not become overly concerned about distracting thoughts. When you realize that your mind is wandering, return to the exercise without criticizing yourself. Try not to force the relaxation response, because this may hinder achievement of the response.

## BASIC RELAXATION POSITIONS

When you are learning or practicing total body relaxation exercises, it is important to assume a comfortable position—one that will not hinder relaxation, cause muscular tension, invite cramps, or provoke unnecessary movement or effects. Most of the following suggestions should be helpful as you try the various positions for relaxation. Some of these suggestions may not apply to you. Adjust the positions to meet your needs and preferences.

1. Find a comfortable position in which you feel a minimum of muscular tension—one that provides environmental support for the body. (Environmental support is the support the body receives from whatever it is resting on. For example, if you are sitting in a chair, your trunk is supported by the seat and back of the chair, your arms are supported by the arms of the chair, and your feet and legs are supported by the floor.) This decreases the amount of muscular tension needed to maintain that position. When muscular tension is reduced, relaxation during the early stages of the learning process is enhanced, and it will be easier for you to achieve the desired relaxation effect.

After the exercises are learned and perfected in positions that provide maximum support, it may be advantageous to practice them in positions in which the body has less support. As you get better at relaxing in positions with less support, you will begin to be able to elicit a relaxed state in almost any environment—on a bus or an airplane, at the office, in a waiting room, riding in a car, on a park bench.

2. The body should be properly aligned. In most of the positions discussed, the right side of the body is aligned with the left side. This allows greater stability when in a deeply relaxed state.

3. Your arms and legs should be supported so that you experience minimal muscular tension. Again, the greater the support, the easier it is to learn the basic exercises.

4. Your hands and arms should not be crossed or touching, nor should the feet and legs. Body parts that touch or rub may cause friction, hot spots, sweating, impaired circulation, and cramping. When limbs cross or touch, they distract from relaxation.

5. You should choose the position or adjustment of a position to meet your own particular needs.

## Positions with Maximum Support

The positions discussed below provide maximum support and comfort. The more support the body has, the less muscular tension is needed to maintain the body in the position. When muscular tension is reduced, you can concentrate better on the relaxation exercises. The positions that provide maximum muscular support include the easy chair position, the supine position, and the side position.

**Easy Chair Position**   The easy chair position is also called the passive sitting position and is an easily recognized position that provides a great deal of support (see Figure 5-1). To assume this position, sit in a high-back chair, lean against the back of the chair, and rest your head against the top or the back of the chair. Your arms can rest on the arms of the chair or on your thighs. Your legs should not be crossed, and your feet should be flat on the floor, comfortably apart. Adjust the position to meet your needs so that you are comfortable and well supported.

FIGURE 5-1
*The Easy Chair Position*

**Supine Position**   The supine position is another commonly used position that provides maximum support (see Figure 5-2). To assume this position, lie down on your back with your arms resting comfortably at the sides and your elbows slightly bent. Your hands should be near your buttocks or thighs. Your legs should be extended (not crossed), with the feet pointing upward and outward in a comfortable, relaxed manner. As you get more relaxed, your feet are likely to fall further apart. Many people are comfortable with the head flat; some prefer to have the head and shoulders propped up or to have a small towel or pillow under the neck, so that the chin is elevated. Do not use a large pillow under the head, as this can cause stiffness in the neck and create muscular tension. For many people, a large pillow can be the cause of headaches.

FIGURE 5-2

*Supine Position*

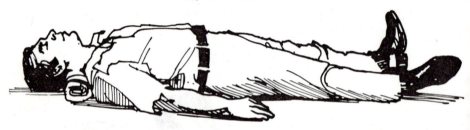

**Supine Position with Arm and Shoulder Risers**   One variation of the supine position is the supine position with arm and shoulder risers (see Figure 5-3). To assume this position, place pillows or blankets under your shoulders and arms to eliminate muscular tension and stretching in the chest region. This position is often used following a mastectomy.

FIGURE 5-3

*Supine Position with Arm and Shoulder Risers*

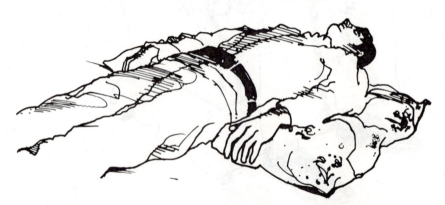

**Supine Position with Knee Risers and with Chair Support of the Lower Leg** Individuals who are swaybacked or have low back pain may need to have their knees elevated to reduce the tension in the lower back. The supine position with knee risers is an adjustment that can be accomplished by placing a pillow or several blankets under the knees to elevate them (see Figure 5-4). The supine position with chair support of the lower leg is assumed by placing your lower legs on the seat of a chair that is drawn close to your buttocks. The appropriate height of the chair is determined by what is most comfortable. Again, comfort and support are your goals.

FIGURE 5-4
*Supine Position with Knee Risers and*
*with Chair Support of the Lower Legs*

**Side Position** Another variation of the supine position is the side position (called the unconscious position in first-aid literature) (see Figure 5-5). Other position variations include lying on the stomach and whatever position is used when going to sleep. Whichever position you use, try to learn the exercises in that position and try not to change your position too frequently.

FIGURE 5-5
*Side Position*

**Positions with Minimum Support**

After you learn the basic relaxation exercises, then practice them in positions in which the body has minimum support. The exercises may be more difficult to do in these less than ideal positions, but proficiency in these positions allows you to make the transition from an ideal environment to more ordinary settings. The most commonly used positions in this category are the coachman's position (forward leaning) and the coachman's position (upright).

**Coachman's Position—Leaning Forward** The forward-leaning coachman's position (see Figure 5-6) is often referred to as the "active sitting position," because a person must actively contract many muscles to maintain the position. The advantage of practicing skills in this position is that the position can be assumed in a variety of places, because it can be used without a back support.

To assume this position, sit on a seat of a bench or chair, exhale, and slowly lean forward and rest your lower arms on your thighs. Arms and hands should not touch each other. The elbows should be bent comfortably. Feet should be flat on the floor and spread comfortably. Allow your head to hang down to a position that is comfortable.

FIGURE 5-6
*Coachman's Position (Leaning Forward)*

If you have trouble finding a comfortable position for your head while it is hanging forward, slowly lean back and bring your head more upright. Continue back until you find the most comfortable position. Keep in mind that this position will require muscular tension, and you may not feel relaxed the first few times you try it. However, if you keep practicing, you will be completely relaxed in this position within a week.

**Coachman's Position—Upright**   The upright coachman's position (see Figure 5-7) does not require as much muscular tension as the leaning coachman's position, because the back is supported. To assume the upright coachman's position, sit on a chair, lean back, and allow the chair to support your body at the buttocks and the back. Arms and hands can rest on the thighs or on the arms of the chair, if the chair has arms and is comfortable. Your feet should be flat on the floor and spread comfortably. The head can hang forward, or it

FIGURE 5-7
*Coachman's Position (Upright)*

can be held upright and balanced comfortably. Variations and adjustments can be made until you are comfortable. Keep in mind that this is a position with minimal muscular support. You will experience more muscular tension in this position than in the positions in which you have maximum support. You may not feel as relaxed the first few times you practice in this position, but with practice you will be completely relaxed in this position within a week.

## SUMMARY

Stress is normal and desirable. However, if we experience too much stress and it begins to dominate our lives and create problems, we need to deal with the stress. To do this, we must make a commitment to a healthy life style. Health must become an important consideration as we plan our daily activities and assume responsibility for our lives.

The basic elements conducive to learning relaxation exercises are a quiet environment, a comfortable position for performing each exercise, a passive attitude while performing exercises, and acceptance of the body's response without "pushing" toward deep relaxation.

Basic relaxation positions that are comfortable are important for achieving deep relaxation. Positions in which the body has maximum support are generally the best positions for learning exercises. It is more difficult to learn the skills in positions in which the body has minimal support, but when you practice relaxation exercises in these positions, you can learn to relax in many different places. The positions used during relaxation should be chosen by the person performing the exercises.

## References

Jencks, Beata. *Exercise Manual for J. H. Schultz's Standard Autogenic Training and Special Formulas.* Salt Lake City: Private Printing, 1973.

Ranta, P. *Exercises and Positions for the Finnish Olympic Ski Jumping Team.* Explained in private conversation, September, 1977.

Schultz, J. H. *Das Autogenic Training.* G. Thieme Verlag, Leipzig, 1932 (12th edition, 1966).

White, John, and Fadiman, James. *Relax: How You Can Feel Better, Reduce Stress and Overcome Tension.* New York: Confucian Press, 1976.

# 6

![black rectangle]

# SENSORY
# AWARENESS
# TRAINING

If a relaxation program is to be effective, a solid foundation must be laid. Sensory awareness training provides the basic building blocks for the next part of a holistic relaxation program. The purpose of this chapter is twofold: (1) to provide information about sensory awareness; and (2) to help you to heighten awareness of your body, throughout the day, through the use of sensory awareness exercises.

## WHAT IS SENSORY AWARENESS?

Sensory awareness is an increased consciousness of sensory perceptions and sensations. Here, we use sensory perception and sensation interchangeably. Both refer to messages from the body and to generalized feelings that are perceived at a conscious level. These include specific messages such as muscular tension, pressure, temperature change, and twitching, and vague feelings such as happiness, peace, contentment, patience, comfort, and security.

In modern society, each individual each day is bombarded with a multitude of stimuli. The mind receives a constant flow of information in the form of sensory input from the eyes, ears, and other organs and tissues of the body. Many of these stimuli demand conscious attention. As we mature, our minds become crowded with thoughts of our external environment and survival within it. We focus on goals, needs, relationships, jobs, and chores.

Unfortunately, our thoughts turn outward and we become less consciously aware of our bodies. Sensory awareness becomes dulled and is ignored.

The purpose of sensory awareness training is to reverse this process and heighten our awareness of our bodies, so that we consciously tune into our bodies and perceive the reactions of our bodies to both internal and external events or stimuli. Sensory awareness training helps us become more aware of a wide range of sensory perceptions and the sensations that accompany them. Sensory awareness training helps us develop a keen observation of sensations in the body that usually do not reach our consciousness. It is a retraining of mind/body connections.

Sensory awareness training is a basic component of a relaxation program. It helps us to perceive a wide range of sensations in our bodies and to recognize tension and relaxation as opposites and to differentiate between them. As we become more aware of the differences in these feelings, we can use relaxation exercises to induce the relaxed state.

## COMMON SENSATIONS

Sensory awareness training can be done while you are active (walking, standing, or running) or passive (sitting or lying down with your eyes closed). The sensations experienced will differ, depending on body position, level of physical activity during the exercise, and level of consciousness. Most of the exercises in this chapter are done in a passive state, and so the sensations you experience will be limited. However, a passive state allows for minimum distractions and deeper concentration during the exercises.

The sensations most easily identified and recognized early in sensory awareness training include heaviness, warmth, calmness (slowing down or patience), sinking down, a general sense of letting go, and monotony. Others include hardness, movement in the body, pressure, rising muscular tension, invigoration, twitching, a conscious awareness of the heartbeat or pulse or a thumping feeling in various body parts.

## HOW TO USE THE EXERCISES

Before performing an exercise, first read the exercise description several times so that you can do the exercise without referring to the text. After you have done the exercise, turn to the Practice Schedule Chart for that exercise and read the goal. The goal is the *minimum* number of times you need to practice that exercise before moving on to the next exercise. Record the date, the amount of time you practice, and your evaluation on the Practice Schedule Chart.

If you have difficulty learning an exercise, you may want to practice that exercise for several days before moving on to the next one. Remember, the exercises are presented in a progressive sequence. Each exercise prepares you for the one that follows.

## SENSORY AWARENESS EXERCISES

Sensory awareness exercises heighten conscious awareness of sensations within the body. They are intended to help you perceive consciously a variety of thoughts, sensations, and feelings related to tension and relaxation. In addition, these exercises can help you to establish the habit of tuning into your body by means of sensory awareness and to develop a pattern of recall, so that the sensations can be consciously recalled when desired.

The exercises presented here are: (1) hand clench, for hand and arm awareness; (2) the stand, for leg, foot, and buttock awareness; and (3) body search, for trunk awareness. Read each exercise description several times before performing the exercise, so that you can perform the exercise without referring to the text. Then perform the exercise with your eyes closed.

### Exercise 1: Hand Clench

The hand clench can be learned easily in any basic position (see Chapter 5) in which you have maximum support and in which you can comfortably keep your eyes closed so that you are not distracted. After the exercise has been learned, it can be done in any position with the eyes open or closed.

Exercise Description
- Assume the desired position (see Chapter 5) and close your eyes.
- Turn your attention to your breathing rhythm and listen to yourself breathe for three to five breaths.
- Clench one hand tightly into a fist, as shown in Figure 6-1, and feel the tension in the muscles of the hand, fingers, and forearms. Immediately begin to open your fist slowly as you relax the fingers, palm, and forearm.
- Focus your attention on the movements, feelings, and sensations in your fingers, palm, and forearm. These sensations may include, but are not limited to, slight movement of each finger, jerking move-

FIGURE 6-1
*The Fist*

ments, tingling, warmth, coolness, and difficulty opening the hand. Feel, sense, and think about each sensation you perceive.

- When your hand is relaxed, your fingers will be slightly curled (Figure 6-2). Think about the relaxed hand for several breaths (about ten to twelve seconds).
- Now extend your fingers and wrist (Figure 6-2). Focus your attention on the wrist, back of the fingers, and the hand. Slowly relax the hand to its normal, comfortable, tension-free position (Figure 6-3).
- As you perform the movement of relaxing the hand from the extended position, try to identify as many sensations and feelings as you can.
- When the hand is in the relaxed position, focus your attention on the feeling opposite of muscular tension—relaxation. Try to identify and sense this relaxed feeling for thirty seconds to a minute.

This entire exercise should take from three to four minutes. The time will vary as you increase your sensory awareness. Repeat this exercise at least three times each day for three days. Record each practice session on the

FIGURE 6-2
*The Fist — Slightly Curled*

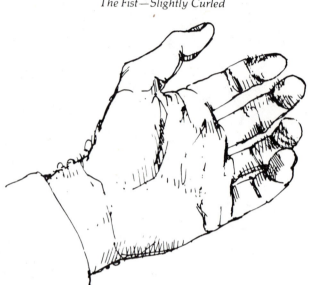

Practice Schedule Chart. Although you may feel relaxed during or following this exercise, keep in mind that this is not a relaxation exercise—it is a sensory awareness exercise. It is designed to help you tune into your body and prepare for the relaxation exercises.

Practice Schedule Chart
Exercise 1: Hand Clench

Goal:  To perform the hand clench exercise during each of three sessions.

| Session | Date Performed | Exercise Time | Evaluation |
|---------|----------------|---------------|------------|
| 1 | | | |
| 2 | | | |
| 3 | | | |

Total time spent on this exercise: _____

FIGURE 6-3
*Extended Fist and Wrist*

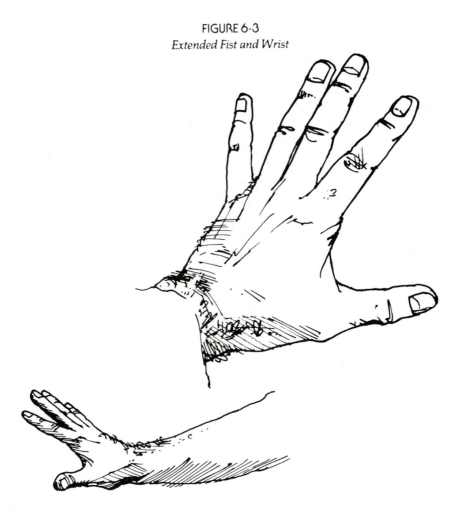

## Exercise 2: The Stand

Standing sensory awareness is begun after at least three practice sessions of the hand clench exercise. The stand should be practiced at least three times, or until learned. The hand clench exercise can be practiced along with the stand during each session.

### Exercise Description

- To perform the standing sensory awareness exercise, stand erect with your eyes open.

- Focus your attention on an object or point four to six feet in front of you.
- With your eyes open, begin concentrating on the lower part of your body—from the waist down.
- Focus your attention on your buttocks. Sense any and all movements in this part of your body, as different muscles tense and relax to help you maintain the standing position and your balance.
- In sequence, move your attention to your thighs (upper legs), knees, calves (lower legs), ankles, feet, and toes.
- As you concentrate on each segment for fifteen to thirty seconds, try to identify all sensations, feelings, and movements in these muscle groups.
- After you have concentrated on each segment of the body, scan the lower part of your body for various sensations and movements. Do this for an additional 30–40 seconds.

The standing exercise can be performed with the eyes closed for greater concentration. However, when doing it with the eyes closed, several precautions should be taken so that you do not lose your balance. To protect yourself from falling, do the exercise while holding onto a table, chair back, door, or other item that provides support (see Figure 6-4). If someone is

FIGURE 6-4
*Standing Support*

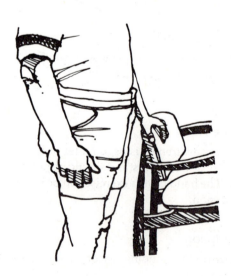

FIGURE 6-5
*Standing with Spotter*

available to help you, that person can be a spotter. A spotter stands close to you as you practice and can intervene if you lose your balance. You should be able to trust this person completely, so you can focus on the exercise and sensations. Figure 6-5 illustrates where a spotter can stand for this exercise.

Remember, the stand should be done a minimum of three times. Record the three practice sessions in the Practice Schedule Chart.

Practice Schedule Chart

Exercise 2: The Stand

Goal:　To practice the stand exercise during each of three sessions (the hand clench exercise can also be practiced during these sessions).

| Session | Date Performed | Exercise Time | Evaluation |
|---------|----------------|---------------|------------|
| 1 | | | |
| 2 | | | |
| 3 | | | |

Total time spent on this exercise: _____

## Exercise 3: Body Search

After learning the stand, add the body search exercise to your repertoire of sensory awareness exercises. This exercise can be practiced with the hand clench and the stand during sensory awareness training.

You may want to abbreviate or shorten the hand clench and standing to spend more time on the body search. The body search introduced here focuses on increasing sensory awareness in the trunk region of the body. The body search exercise takes about two to three minutes.

Exercise Description

- Sit quietly in the position desired and listen to yourself breathe for three or four breaths.
- Turn your attention to the trunk region of your body. Scan the trunk; locate and identify any movement in this area. Movements you may identify include, but are not limited to, heartbeats, stomach adjustments, diaphragm movements, peristalsis, twitching, and chest expansion.
- Once you locate a movement, try to feel and experience it.
- After you have identified movements within the trunk region, scan the trunk region again but this time for stillness (lack of movement). When stillness is identified, think about and experience that stillness and then compare this feeling to those associated with movements.

- Continue the exercise for two to three minutes.
- Record each session in the Practice Schedule Chart.

Practice Schedule Chart
Exercise 3: Body Search

Goal:  To perform the body search exercise during each of three sessions (the hand clench and the stand can also be practiced during each session).

| Session | Date Performed | Exercise Time | Evaluation |
|---------|----------------|---------------|------------|
| 1 | | | |
| 2 | | | |
| 3 | | | |

Total time spent on this exercise: _____

## SUMMARY

In modern society, we often are so occupied with thoughts of our external environment that we become almost oblivious to what is happening within our bodies. Our bodies are continually providing us with feedback, but we must become aware of this feedback if it is to be useful. Sensory awareness training is designed to help us tune into our bodies. Sensory awareness is an increased consciousness of sensory perceptions.

The hand clench and standing exercises described in this chapter allow the individual to become aware of sensations in the limbs. The body search exercise helps a person to tune into sensations in the trunk. These are basic prerelaxation exercises in the holistic relaxation program and prepare you to move to Chapter 7, where the breathing rhythms that build on this base are discussed.

**Reference**

Jencks, Beata. *Respiration for Relaxation, Invigoration, and Special Accomplishments.* Salt Lake City: Private Printing, 1974.

# 7

---

# BREATHING RHYTHMS

Breathing rhythms are related to relaxation. In this chapter we examine the various sensations related to breath inhalation, pause, and exhalation. Major emphasis is on the exhalation phase, which is the relaxation phase. In Chapter 8, the sensations associated with the exhalation phase are coupled with supporting environment exercises to provide the basis of many relaxation skills.

## BREATHING RHYTHMS

A close relationship exists between an individual's intellectual and emotional state and his or her breathing rhythm. A sudden idea, excitement, fear, anxiety, anger, hostility, or fright may cause us to hold our breath, inhale, or begin to breathe rapidly. When this happens, the free swinging of the diaphragm has been inhibited by a thought or an emotion.

The breathing rhythm can be broken down and discussed in three distinct phases: inhalation, pause, and exhalation. These phases produce various sensations that are important to the holistic relaxation program.

### Inhalation

The inhalation phase of the breathing rhythm is the tension-producing phase. The importance of the inhalation phase is often overlooked in relaxation programs, but it is important for several reasons. First, the inhalation phase is used to come out of a relaxed state. As we awaken from a deep sleep or a relaxed state, we usually yawn, stretch, and take a deep breath simultaneously. This combination, which centers around deep inhalation, produces muscular tension. That muscular tension in turn provides a feeling of invigoration, refreshment, mental stimulation, and alertness. The inhalation phase promotes both physical and mental invigoration. Second, the inhalation phase is important because it evokes many feelings that are helpful in developing a keen observation of sensory awareness. Many of these sensations are the opposite of the sensations associated with the exhalation phase. These sensations are identified in Table 7-1.[1]

### Exercise 4: Inhalation

To perform the inhalation exercise, focus only on the inhalation phase of the breathing rhythm. Disregard the exhalation phase and the pauses in the breathing rhythm.

Caution: When performing this exercise, do not hyperventilate. Hyperventilation is a condition that results from carbon dioxide depletion. It is caused by forced respirations—increased inspiration and expiration of air resulting from increased rate or depth of respiration, or both.

TABLE 7-1
*Inhalation Sensations*

- Invigoration
- Increased tension
- Coolness
- Hardness
- Dryness
- Expansion (chest region)
- Tightening
- Upward body movement; ascending; levitating
- Alertness; awakening
- Gasping; speeding; being startled
- Refreshment
- Preparation for action

Adapted from Beata Jencks, *Your Body: Biofeedback at Its Best* (Chicago: Nelson Hall, 1977), pp. 136–137.

Allow a natural pause after each inhalation and exhalation to take place and be sure to exhale fully. If you feel light-headed or dizzy, a ringing or buzzing in the ears, or a trembling feeling, discontinue the exercise immediately. These are warning signs of hyperventilation.

## Exercise Description

- Sit upright in a chair with your eyes closed.
- Take a breath as you concentrate on the inhalation phase and the sensation you want to observe (from Table 7-1).
- Exhale, but do not think about the exhalation. Simply allow your body to exhale on its own accord.
- Focus all of your attention on the inhalation phase. Repeat the inhalation three to four times, concentrating and feeling any of the sensations listed in Table 7-1. Again, disregard the exhalations.
- Let yourself experience each feeling, action, or image for several breaths.
- Record your practice session on the Practice Schedule Chart.

Practice Schedule Chart
Exercise 4: Inhalation

Goal:  To perform the inhalation exercise during each of three sessions.

| Session | Date Performed | Exercise Time | Evaluation |
|---------|----------------|---------------|------------|
| 1 | | | |
| 2 | | | |
| 3 | | | |

Total time spent on this exercise: _____

## Exhalation

The exhalation phase of the breathing rhythm is the relaxation phase. During exhalation you let go of the tension that developed in the body naturally from the inhalation, or tension-producing phase. The exhalation phase is, in es-

TABLE 7-2
*Sensations Related to Exhalations*

---

- Heaviness
- Sinking down; descending; falling asleep
- Warmth
- Slowing down; patience
- Boredom
- Relaxed feeling; letting go; release of tension
- Lengthening of breathing
- Comfort; contentment

---

Adapted from Beata Jencks, *Your Body: Biofeedback at Its Best* (Chicago: Nelson Hall, 1977), pp. 136–137.

sence, the built-in mechanism for relaxation that everyone has. The exhalation phase is normally felt as a downward movement. The downward movement is felt because the muscles relax and you sink down because of gravity.

The exhalation phase of the breathing rhythm is emphasized in many of the relaxation exercises. In fact, the exhalation phase is the foundation for many of the relaxation exercises used in this holistic relaxation program.

Table 7-2 lists many of the sensations identified with the exhalation phase of the breathing rhythm. As you can see, many of these sensations are the opposite of the sensations of the inhalation phase. The following exercise focuses on feelings associated with (and commonly felt during) the exhalation phase of the breathing rhythm.

## Exercise 5: Exhalation

The sensations commonly associated with the exhalation phase of the breathing rhythm (Table 7-2) can be easily identified and sensed. Focus your concentration on the exhalation phase of the breathing rhythm and disregard the inhalation phase. Remember to breathe normally, to let your body breathe by itself, and not to extend the exhalation phase.

### Exercise Description

- Sit upright in a chair with the eyes closed.
- Breathe normally while focusing your attention on your breathing rhythm. Listen to yourself breathe for three or four breathing cycles.

- After listening for three or four cycles, focus your attention inward and concentrate on the exhalation phase of the breathing rhythm and the sensation you would like to observe (from Table 7-2).
- Focus on the sensation only during the exhalation phase of the breathing rhythm. Do not think about the inhalation at all—just allow your body to inhale when it desires.
- *Do not prolong the exhalations*—just allow the body to breathe.
- Example: Each time you exhale, try to feel heaviness as you are breathing out. Allow your mind to go blank during the inhalations. Feel the heaviness again as you exhale. You may feel this heaviness in the head, the neck, the trunk, arms, hands, fingers, legs, buttocks, feet—anywhere. Just feel heaviness somewhere as you exhale. Concentrate, but allow the heaviness to happen.
- After you feel and experience heaviness during the exhalation phase for several breathing cycles, terminate the exercise by flexing, stretching, taking a deep breath, and opening your eyes. Record any observed sensations on the Practice Schedule Charts under Evaluation.
- Remember: Do not try to force the sensations. Perform the exercises regularly. When your body is ready, you will consciously notice the sensations. Maintain a passive attitude at all times.

Practice Schedule Chart
Exercise 5: Exhalation

Goal:   To perform the exhalation exercise during each of three sessions.

| Session | Date Performed | Exercise Time | Evaluation |
|---------|----------------|---------------|------------|
| 1 | | | |
| 2 | | | |
| 3 | | | |

Total time spent on this exercise: _____

## Holding the Breath

Holding your breath can occur in a variety of situations. Two of the most common situations are discussed here. We may hold our breaths when we are

TABLE 7-3
*Sensations Related to Holding the Breath*
*Following Inhalation*

- Maintaining or increasing tension
- Maintaining or increasing pressure
- Nervous tension
- Uneasiness or unsteadiness
- Strained attention
- Rigidity
- Rising up
- Holding on

Adapted from Beata Jencks, *Your Body: Biofeedback at Its Best*
(Chicago: Nelson Hall, 1977), pp. 136–137.

confronted with sudden, unexpected stressors. When this happens, we usually take deep, sudden inhalations, and the sensations felt are tension-related. This sudden inhalation usually occurs unconsciously and is accompanied by increased blood pressure. The sensations that can be identified and felt with the holding of the breath following an inhalation are listed in Table 7-3. Also, we may, for various reasons, hold our breaths consciously, usually for particular reasons. Occasionally this is done following an inhalation—for example, by a person swimming underwater. The sensations felt when this is done are the same as in Table 7-3. If we consciously hold our breath after an exhalation, the sensations felt are those listed in Table 7-4. These sensations are similar to those experienced during a relaxed state. We are likely to hold our breaths following exhalation when we require a relaxed state or stillness; for example, when shooting a free throw in basketball. This is commonly done in various sports and in the performing arts, including dance.

TABLE 7-4
*Sensations Related to Holding the Breath*
*Following Exhalation*

- A pause
- Stopping or stillness
- A relaxed state
- Sinking down

Adapted from Beata Jencks, *Your Body: Biofeedback at Its Best*
(Chicago: Nelson Hall, 1977), pp. 136–137.

## Exercise 6: Holding the Breath Following Inhalation

An exercise for holding the breath following inhalation is done to increase sensory awareness. While performing this exercise, you should try to experience the sensations listed in Table 7-3. Note each sensation that you feel. Holding the breath following an inhalation is done first. Holding the breath following an exhalation is done second.

Caution: If for medical reasons you should not hold your breath, do not perform this exercise.

### Exercise Description

- Sit upright in a chair or stool in one of the recommended positions.
- Passively observe your breathing rhythm for three or four breathing cycles.
- Following passive observation of the breathing cycle, inhale deeply and concentrate on a sensation you have selected.
- Hold your breath for three to five seconds (be sure you hold your breath only for a length of time that is comfortable for you).
- Focus on feeling a sensation from Table 7-3. After feeling the selected sensation (or attempting to feel it) two or three times, move on to a different sensation from Table 7-3 and repeat the sequence.
- If you do not feel the sensation after attempting to observe it for three or four breaths, move on to a different sensation. Remember: You cannot force awareness of a sensation. Maintain a passive attitude.
- Record any sensations observed on the Practice Schedule Chart.

### Practice Schedule Chart
Exercise 6: Holding the Breath Following Inhalation

Goal:   To perform the exercise during each of three sessions.

| Session | Date Performed | Exercise Time | Evaluation |
|---------|---------------|---------------|------------|
| 1       |               |               |            |
| 2       |               |               |            |
| 3       |               |               |            |

Total time spent on this exercise: _____

## Exercise 7: Holding the Breath Following Exhalation

### Exercise Description

- Sit upright in a chair or stool in one of the recommended positions.
- Passively observe your breathing rhythm for three or four breathing cycles.
- On the third or fourth breath, concentrate on feeling the sensation you selected from Table 7-4. At the end of the exhalation (during the pause), hold your breath and feel the sensation you have selected. Hold the breath for only two to five seconds, depending on what is comfortable for you.
- Once you have observed the sensation, record it on the Practice Schedule Chart and move to a different sensation from Table 7-4.
- Once again, do not force the sensation. Maintain a passive attitude.

Practice Schedule Chart
Exercise 7: Holding the Breath Following Exhalation

Goal:   To perform the exercise during each of three sessions.

| Session | Date Performed | Exercise Time | Evaluation |
|---------|----------------|---------------|------------|
| 1 | | | |
| 2 | | | |
| 3 | | | |

Total time spent on this exercise: _____

## SUMMARY

The breathing rhythm, when used properly, can help us to develop sensory awareness and a relaxed state. Each phase of the breathing rhythm (inhalation, pause, and exhalation) is important when developing increased sensory awareness. Because we are interested here in relaxation, we focus on the exhalation phase, which is the body's built-in relaxation phase.

## Note

1 Beata Jencks, *Respiration for Relaxation, Invigoration, and Special Accomplishments* (Salt Lake City: Private Printing, 1974), p. 3.

## References

Jencks, Beata. *Respiration for Relaxation, Invigoration, and Special Accomplishments.* Salt Lake City: Private Printing, 1974.

Jencks, Beata. *Your Body: Biofeedback at Its Best.* Chicago: Nelson Hall, 1977.

# THE SUPPORTING
# ENVIRONMENT

When learning supporting environment exercises, information from several of the previous chapters is used: the basic positions for relaxation (from Chapter 5), the sensory awareness sensations (from Chapter 6), and the sensations related to the exhalation phase of the breathing rhythm (from Chapter 7).

## WHAT IS THE SUPPORTING ENVIRONMENT?

The supporting environment is the environment around us, the surfaces against which body parts are resting, the environment that supports the body in its current position. A supporting environment exercise helps the individual achieve a comfortable position that involves a minimum of muscular tension. A person who uses supporting environment exercises regularly will be able to achieve a relaxed state quickly. These exercises also help the individual to be aware of muscular tension during normal daily routines and to make adjustments so that muscular tension is decreased. This, in turn, helps to conserve energy so the individual is less tired. Many individuals who have had a history of exhaustion late in the afternoon or early in the evening have reported that the supporting environment exercises are effective in reversing this pattern. They are able to conserve enough energy so that they can be active in the evening.

TABLE 8-1
*Sensations Felt during the*
*Supporting Environment Exercise*

- Sinking downward or descending into the
  supporting environment
- Supporting environment coming up to meet, engulf,
  and support you
- Heaviness
- Relaxation; letting go; release of tension
- Contentment; comfort

## THE BASIC SUPPORTING ENVIRONMENT ROUTINE

The basic routine to follow in performing the supporting environment exercises is simple. First, position yourself so that you are in one of the basic positions described in Chapter 5. These positions give you support, comfort, and good body alignment. Second, focus on your breathing rhythm and listen to yourself breathe for three to four breathing cycles. Third, focus on your body, on a specific part of your body, or on various parts (arms, hands, legs, shoulders). Fourth, during the exhalation phase of your breathing rhythm, concentrate on picking up sensations related to the exhalation phase (relaxation) in the body parts you are observing. And fifth, allow the environment to support your body so that you use a minimum of muscular tension to maintain your position. Table 8-1 lists sensations you can expect to feel.

### Exercise 8: Supporting Environment

To do the supporting environment exercise, make yourself comfortable in the supine position or one of the variations of this position.

### Exercise Description

(Underlined sections should be timed with the exhalation phase of the breathing rhythm.)

- As you lie in the selected supine position, focus your complete attention on your breathing rhythm and listen to yourself breathe for three to six breathing cycles.

- Now focus your attention on your lower legs (feet, ankles, and calves), and as you exhale, feel the lower legs become heavy and sink into the floor or bed. Allow your lower legs to be supported entirely by the supporting environment. Each time you exhale for the next two or three breaths, feel your lower legs become heavy and sink into the environment. Think heaviness and sinking only as you exhale. Time your thoughts of heaviness and sinking with the exhalation phase only. Disregard the inhalations completely.

- Now move your attention to your upper legs (the thigh area) and buttocks. As you exhale, allow your upper legs and buttocks to relax and become heavy and sink into the supporting environment. Simply allow the supporting environment to support your body with little or no help from muscle tension.

- For the next two to three breathing cycles, each time you exhale feel your upper legs and buttocks relax and become heavy and sink into the supporting environment. Once again, concentrate on the sensation of relaxing—letting go, feeling heaviness and sinking as you exhale. Completely disregard the inhalation phase of the breathing rhythm.

- Next, switch your attention to your upper body—trunk, shoulders, head, and neck—and relax and let go as you feel heaviness and sink into the environment as you exhale. Repeat for two to three breaths and allow the environment to support you.

- Now focus your attention on your upper arms, lower arms, wrists, hands, and fingers as you exhale. Allow your arms and hands to relax, let go, and feel heaviness as you allow the supporting surface to support this area.

- For the next three to four breaths, focus on your entire body. As you exhale, feel your body relax, let go, and feel heaviness. Can you feel your body giving up muscular tension? Can you feel the supporting environment come up to your body?

- Just relax your body, allow it to let go. Allow your entire body to be supported by the supporting environment. Allow only minimal muscular tension throughout your body to maintain this position.

- Wait for two to three more breathing cycles and then flex, stretch, take a deep breath, and open your eyes.

As you practice the supporting environment exercises, use the sequence of movements illustrated in Figure 8-1. The sequence includes four basic groups:

1. Lower legs (feet, ankles, calves)
2. Upper legs and buttocks (thighs and buttocks)
3. Upper body (trunk, shoulders, head, and neck)
4  Arms (upper arms, lower arms, hands, and fingers)

FIGURE 8-1
*Supporting Environment Sequence.*

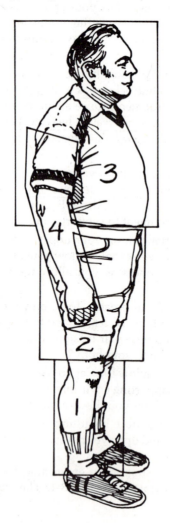

Caution: Do not sit up or stand up too quickly, as you may become dizzy. After the exercise, raise your head and chest and lean on an elbow for a few moments. Then sit up and, once adjusted, slowly stand up. You may want to repeat the flexing and stretching if you do not feel alert immediately after the exercise.

Practice Schedule Chart

Exercise 8: Supporting Environment

Goal:   To perform the exercise during each of three sessions.

| Session | Date Performed | Exercise Time | Evaluation |
|---------|----------------|---------------|------------|
| 1       |                |               |            |
| 2       |                |               |            |
| 3       |                |               |            |

Total time spent on this exercise: _____

## SUMMARY

The supporting environment exercise is designed to help you achieve a comfortable position with a minimum of muscular tension. Supporting environment exercises can be used in finding a comfortable position to help achieve a relaxed state, or you can use them to become more aware of tension throughout the day, so that you can adjust your position to minimize the tension. The basic exercise routine is: (1) find a comfortable, well-supported position; (2) focus on your breathing rhythm; (3) focus on the entire body or a specific part of the body; (4) during exhalation, concentrate on feelings and sensations related to relaxation; and (5) passively allow the environment to support your body, so that a minimum of muscular tension is needed to maintain your position.

### Reference

Jencks, Beata. *Respiration for Relaxation, Invigoration, and Special Accomplishments.* Salt Lake City: Private Printing, 1974.

# PART THREE

# TOTAL BODY RELAXATION

In Part Two, you learned and practiced the foundation exercises for your relaxation program. Although it is possible to experience relaxation with these exercises, the heart of the relaxation program, from which the most physiological benefits are derived, is total body relaxation. Part Three presents several means of eliciting total body relaxation and the accompanying desirable physiological responses.

## WHAT IS TOTAL BODY RELAXATION?

Total body relaxation skills allow the user to withdraw from the immediate environment into the confines of his or her being. Many writers refer to this as achieving the alpha level of consciousness. Others say that total body relaxation enables the individual to get in touch with the soul, making it a transcendental experience. Still others describe the experience in strictly physiological terms that deal with the amount of physical relaxation produced.

You will probably find that the results achieved during total body relaxation are dependent on your intent and on your effectiveness in eliciting the response. Here, the physical and psychological well-being that results from regular practice of total body relaxation techniques will be emphasized. These techniques are but a few of the means that can be used in the wellness process to intervene in the stress cycle or to nourish body and mind.

Many relaxation practitioners promote a single technique for eliciting total body relaxation. Basic to the holistic and wellness approach to relaxation used here is the belief that individuals are different, and that what works and is beneficial for one person may not be desirable for another. Of course, the results achieved are related to the intent and purpose the individual has in mind when selecting a particular technique. It is possible to elicit the relaxation response and accompanying physiological benefits through some activities unrelated to relaxation skills. These other activities include, but are not limited to, meditative prayer, daydreaming, reading, and needlework. Usually, however, the response is elicited by the use of a structured and systematic method requiring practice. These methods include, but are not limited to, transcendental meditation (TM), yoga, progressive relaxation, Benson's method, hypnosis, standard autogenic training, and Silva Mind Control. Any activity in which a person is well supported by the environment and has his or her attention "fixed" for a period of time can provide total body relaxation.

Most total body relaxation techniques elicit the response in one of two ways. Since stress and muscular tension can be generated either from the cerebral cortex through the central nervous system to the various muscle groups or from the various muscles through the central nervous system to the cortex, total body relaxation can be achieved from either end. That is, some total body relaxation techniques (such as transcendental meditation, standard autogenic training, hypnosis, and Benson's method) are effective in reducing the amount of stimuli to the cerebral cortex, thus reducing the central nervous system activity and eventually eliciting a relaxed state. When a person is in a deep relaxation state, there are almost no anxiety-producing stimuli to the cortex, and body metabolism and other physiological processes slow down.

On the other hand, techniques that involve progressive relaxation have their origin in various muscle groups. As a person reduces muscular tension and allows relaxation to develop in the various muscle groups, there is reduced activity through the central nervous system to the cerebral cortex. When stimuli to the cortex are reduced, fewer impulses are fired back to the muscles via the central nervous system. Again, body metabolism slows down, and total body relaxation can be achieved.

Although specific relaxation techniques elicit the relaxation response through different starting points, the routes are basically the same. And so a combination of techniques can also be effective in eliciting the response. It is up to each individual to determine which techniques, or combinations of techniques, are most effective in eliciting the desired response.

It should be emphasized that each technique, or combination of techniques, will work only if practiced regularly. Simply knowing about a technique will not be beneficial in times of anxiety and stress. Nor will knowledge alone help you to become less anxious or to slow down your daily pace. The techniques must be practiced (involvement) on a regular basis (assessment), by you (self-responsibility). As you begin to feel better physically and to develop a more positive outlook (reinforcement), you will feel increasing motivation to continue relaxation techniques. A higher level of health and wellness will be reached—and you will have reached it on your own.

# PROGRESSIVE
# RELAXATION

Progressive relaxation was developed by Edmund Jacobson, a physician, and was first described by him in 1938 in his classic book titled *Progressive Relaxation*. Jacobson became interested in relaxation when he noticed that bed rest, traditionally assigned for various ills, did not always produce the desired results. He observed that even though patients were lying down, or sitting, in a restful position, they still worried, fretted, and contracted their muscles. Progressive relaxation was the term coined by Jacobson as he sought a technique to induce nerve-muscle relaxation in his patients.

Nerve-muscle relaxation was designed to rid the body of residual tension—the very fine, continued contraction of a muscle along with slight movements or reflexes. In simple terms, residual tension is what is left over after an untrained person attempts to relax. Jacobson described residual tension as:

> When a person lies relaxed in the ordinary sense, but not completely relaxed in the physiological sense, the following signs reveal the presence of residual tension: his breathing is slightly irregular in time or force and perhaps he sighs occasionally; his pulse rate may be normal but is likely to be somewhat higher than that shown in later tests; the same is true of his temperature and blood pressure. If you watch him closely, you will see that he is not perfectly quiet, for he makes slight movements at times, wrinkles his forehead slightly, frowns, winks rapidly, contracts muscles about the eyes or moves

the eyeballs under the closed lids, shifts his head, a limb or even a finger. The knee jerk and other deep reflexes can be elicited . . . he starts upon any sudden noise. . . . Finally, his mind continues to be active, and once started, worry or oppressive emotion will persist.[1]

Getting rid of this residual tension is the purpose of progressive relaxation.

Residual tension is reduced by consciously relaxing, in a progressive manner, the skeletal muscle groups of the body. For most of us, especially for those who are overstressed, this involves a retraining process. In the initial learning phase, we try to develop "muscle sense." This is accomplished by consciously creating muscular tension so that we can feel and recognize tenseness. Then we relax our muscles, feeling and experiencing relaxation. As we develop muscle sense, we get better at tuning into our bodies, detecting tension, and intervening with relaxation before muscular tension has spread to other areas of our bodies. In other words, we learn to feel the tenseness develop and to relax before headache, backache, or fatigue develop.

After we have practiced tensing and relaxing the various muscle groups several times and have achieved better muscle sense, the tension phase is eliminated. Then we can concentrate on tuning into each muscle group, feeling, sensing, and experiencing only the relaxation. With practice, we can become so keenly aware of the feelings of muscular relaxation that, even when faced with a stressful situation or series of life events, we can relax.

This technique for relaxing is called *progressive relaxation* for three reasons. First, muscle groups are relaxed more and more with each practice. Second, each of the major muscle groups is relaxed one after the other. As a new muscle group is added, we simultaneously relax the other parts we have already learned to relax. Third, more and more total body relaxation is experienced as we move into the relaxation phase. We progress toward a relaxed state that will be maintained beyond the relaxation period. Thus, the skill is progressive in movement from one muscle group to another and in the extent of body relaxation achieved. This method of relaxation does not produce a hypnotic state or trance.[2]

There are many advantages to using the progressive technique to elicit the relaxation response; for example:

1. The participant doesn't have to put faith in someone or something other than him or her self.
2. There is no need for any special equipment, such as is needed for biofeedback.
3. Relaxation is not chemically induced.
4. It is simple; the participant only needs to learn the routine and practice at regular intervals.

5. The routine is easy to learn because it involves familiar body parts.
6. The technique can be learned in a relatively short time (several weeks) with three daily practice sessions of five minutes each.
7. It can be adapted easily to suit individual needs and preferences.
8. Once an individual has learned progressive relaxation, it can be combined with other relaxation exercises to more effectively elicit total body relaxation.

## BASIC PROGRESSIVE RELAXATION EXERCISES

When performing exercises 9 through 18, your goal should be to use the basic progressive relaxation technique to develop the muscle sense required to identify muscular tension and muscular relaxation. In this chapter you will focus on just one set of muscles during each practice session. You should practice the exercise with those muscles for five to seven minutes per practice session. During the first two sessions, you should use both the contraction and relaxation phases of the exercise. During the third practice session of each day, eliminate the contraction (tenseness) and focus solely on relaxation in the muscles. You will notice that as you progress, tenseness is eliminated in favor of relaxation. At various times while performing the exercises, make mental notes about the sensations you feel. Record these sensations in the Practice Schedule Chart after each exercise.

It is important not to skip a practice session or a muscle group during the time when you are laying the groundwork for total body relaxation.

Read each exercise description several times, until you are certain of what is required. Then perform the exercises. If you feel that nothing happened with the selected muscle group, read the exercise description again to determine if you performed the exercise properly. Make the necessary adjustments and try the exercise again. Be patient. Relaxation will come when your body is ready.

As you progress through the exercises, you will discover that your perception of time changes. What seems like just a couple of minutes may actually be ten minutes. We suggest that you practice the exercises only when you are not rushed. Worrying about time or an appointment can interfere with the elicitation of the response.

## Exercise 9: Right Arm

### Exercise Description

- Assume the desired relaxation position and close your eyes.
- Tune into the exhalation phase of your breathing. Feel the warmth of that breath and r-e-l-a-x as you exhale, and r-e-l-a-x as you exhale.
- Focus your attention on the supporting environment. As you continue to tune into your exhalations, allow your muscles to relax and to become a part of that supporting surface. Exhale and sink into that supporting environment.
- Now turn your mental attention to your right forearm—to the top area between your wrist and elbow. Very slowly, moving the hand only at the wrist joint, raise the hand upward and backward, creating muscular tension in this group of muscles. Do not rush to feel the tension, just experience the tension as you feel it (Figure 9-1). Feel, sense, and experience the muscular tension.
- As your hand becomes fully extended backward and the muscles are fully contracted, hold for a second or two, exhale, and—with each exhalation and only on the exhalation—slowly return that hand to a resting position, feeling the relaxation in the muscle group.
- Stop your movement with each inhalation and begin again with each new exhalation. Continue to focus your attention on the feelings of relaxation for several breaths after the hand is resting in the normal position.

FIGURE 9-1
*Progressive Relaxation of Arms*

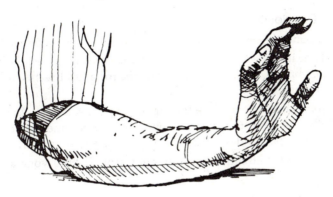

- Repeat the entire process again, focusing on the same forearm. Especially note the sensations of relaxation.
- When fully relaxed, make a comparison between your right arm and your left arm. Keep attention on your right arm and permit your entire body to relax with each exhalation for six to ten breaths.
- When ready, flex-stretch-inhale and open your eyes. Feel the invigoration.
- Record your sensations in the Practice Schedule Chart.

Practice Schedule Chart
Exercise 9: Right Arm

Goal:   To develop the feelings of, first, muscle tension, and then of muscle relaxation during each of three sessions.

| Session | Date Performed | Exercise Time | Evaluation |
|---------|----------------|---------------|------------|
| 1       |                |               |            |
| 2       |                |               |            |
| 3       |                |               |            |

Total time spent on this exercise: _____

## Exercise 10: Left Arm

Exercise Description

- Assume the desired relaxation position and close your eyes.
- Tune into the exhalation phase of your breathing, feel the warmth of that breath, listen to yourself breathe for a few breaths, and r-e-l-a-x as you exhale.
- Focus your attention on the supporting environment. As you exhale, allow yourself to feel that support as you become a part of the support. Exhale and sink into the supporting environment.
- Turn your attention to your right arm. Picture your arm on that

supporting surface and relax the muscles with each of the next ten exhalations.

- Without opening your eyes, shift your attention to the left arm. Very slowly (and moving the hand only at the wrist joint), raise the hand upward and backward, creating muscular tension in the forearm group of muscles. Feel, sense, and experience this muscular tension.
- As your hand becomes fully extended backward and the muscles are fully contracted, hold for a second or two, exhale, and, with each exhalation and only on the exhalation, slowly return the left hand to a resting position, feeling the relaxation in the muscle group as you go.
- Stop your movement with the inhalation, and begin again with the exhalation. Continue to focus your attention on the feelings of relaxation for several breaths after the hand is resting in the normal position.
- Repeat the process (the tension phase) again, noting specifically the sensations of relaxation. When fully relaxed, make a comparison between your left and right arms.
- As you focus on the relaxation developing in both arms, permit your entire body to relax as you exhale. Let your muscles go and relax for one to two minutes.
- When ready, flex-stretch-inhale and open your eyes.
- Record your sensations in the Practice Schedule Chart.

Practice Schedule Chart
Exercise 10: Left Arm

Goal:   To develop the feelings of muscle tension and muscle relaxation during each of three sessions.

| Session | Date Performed | Exercise Time | Evaluation |
|---------|---------------|---------------|------------|
| 1 | | | |
| 2 | | | |
| 3 | | | |

Total time spent on this exercise: _____

### Exercise 11: Neck and Shoulders

Exercise Description

- Assume your desired relaxation position, close your eyes, and begin listening to yourself breathe; r-e-l-a-x as you exhale.
- Allow the supporting environment to support your body; r-e-l-a-x as you exhale.
- Focus your attention on the muscles in the lower back of your neck and the area between your shoulder blades.
- Slowly raise only your shoulders upward toward your ears and slightly backward, creating muscular tension between your shoulder blades and in the lower neck region (Figure 9-2). Hold this for one to two seconds and then, in time with only your exhalations, slowly return your shoulders to their normal position.
- Feel and experience the relaxation develop in these muscles. Remember to move only with the exhalations.
- Continue to focus on this part of the body and the relaxation. Should your thoughts begin to wonder, passively disregard them and return to experiencing the relaxation.

FIGURE 9-2

*Progressive Relaxation of Neck and Shoulders*

- After one to two minutes and when ready, flex-stretch-inhale and open your eyes.
- Perform the tension phase with this group of muscles once during each of three practice sessions.
- Record your sensations in the Practice Schedule Chart.

Practice Schedule Chart
Exercise 11: Neck and Shoulders

Goal:   To develop the feelings of muscle tension and muscle relaxation in shoulder and neck areas during each of three sessions.

| Session | Date Performed | Exercise Time | Evaluation |
|---------|----------------|---------------|------------|
| 1 | | | |
| 2 | | | |
| 3 | | | |

Total time spent on this exercise: _____

## Exercise 12: Combination

Exercise Description

- Assume your desired relaxation position, close your eyes, listen to yourself breathe, and feel the warmth of the exhalation. R-e-l-a-x as you exhale.
- Focus your attention on the supporting environment, permit your body to be totally supported by that surface, and r-e-l-a-x as you exhale.
- Focus your attention between your shoulder blades and lower neck muscles and relax these muscles more and more with each exhalation. Continue to relax these muscles for one to two minutes.
- Now focus your attention on your right arm. With each exhalation, relax in succession the thumb, index finger, middle finger, ring finger, little finger, hand, wrist, forearm, elbow, and upper arm. Feel, sense, and experience the relaxation developing in your right arm.

- Next focus your attention on your left arm and follow the same sequence as with the right arm, relaxing each part as you exhale.
- As you focus on the relaxation developing further and further in your arms, shoulders, and neck regions, permit your entire body to relax as you exhale.
- When ready, flex-stretch-inhale and open your eyes.
- Stay in your relaxation position for a few more breaths until your body feels invigorated and ready to return to your normal activity.
- Record your sensations in the Practice Schedule Chart.

Practice Schedule Chart
Exercise 12: Combination

Goal:  To feel, sense, and experience relaxation in the hands, arms, neck, and shoulder muscles during each of three sessions.

| Session | Date Performed | Exercise Time | Evaluation |
|---------|----------------|---------------|------------|
| 1 | | | |
| 2 | | | |
| 3 | | | |

Total time spent on this exercise: _____

## Exercise 13: Mouth and Cheeks

Exercise Description

- Assume your desired relaxation position, close your eyes, and begin listening to yourself breathe. R-e-l-a-x as you exhale.
- Allow the supporting environment to support your body; r-e-l-a-x as you exhale and sink into that environment.
- Focus your attention on your nose, cheeks, and throat area for several breaths.

FIGURE 9-3
*Progressive Relaxation of Mouth and Cheeks*

- Pucker your nose tightly by lifting your front lip upward and then open your mouth and extend the corners of your mouth toward your cheeks as much as you can.
- Hold for one or two seconds and then, in time with your exhalations, slowly return these muscles to a relaxed position (Figure 9-3).
- Focus on the relaxation as you check to be sure your jaw is resting comfortably and you are not gritting your teeth.
- After one to two minutes, flex-stretch-inhale and open your eyes.
- Record your sensations in the Practice Schedule Chart.

Practice Schedule Chart

Exercise 13: Mouth and Cheeks

Goal:   To develop the feelings of muscle tension and muscle relaxation in the muscles of the nose, mouth, and throat during each of three sessions.

| Session | Date Performed | Exercise Time | Evaluation |
|---------|----------------|---------------|------------|
| 1 | | | |
| 2 | | | |
| 3 | | | |

Total time spent on this exercise: _____

## Exercise 14: Eyes

Exercise Description

- Assume the desired relaxation position, close your eyes, and tune into your exhalations for a few breaths. As you exhale, r-e-l-a-x and r-e-l-a-x and r-e-l-a-x.
- For several exhalations, check your jaws to be sure they are resting comfortably.
- Check your cheeks to be sure they are relaxed.
- Focus your attention on your eyes for several breaths.
- As you squint, squeeze your eyes tightly (Figure 9-4). Do not hold the tenseness after muscular tension has been generated.
- Exhale and slowly focus on the relaxation that begins to develop in the eyes and surrounding area for six to eight breaths.
- If you still notice movement or tenseness, repeat the squint again while simultaneously creating the tenseness in your right forearm as in Exercise 9.
- As you focus on the relaxation developing in your eyes, feel and experience the relaxation in your entire face for one to two minutes.
- When ready, flex-stretch-inhale and open your eyes.
- Record your sensations in the Practice Schedule Chart.

FIGURE 9-4
*Progressive Relaxation of the Eyes*

Practice Schedule Chart
Exercise 14: Eyes

Goal:   To develop the feelings of muscle tension and muscle relaxation between and around the eyes during each of three sessions.

| Session | Date Performed | Exercise Time | Evaluation |
|---------|----------------|---------------|------------|
| 1       |                |               |            |
| 2       |                |               |            |
| 3       |                |               |            |

Total time spent on this exercise: _____

## Exercise 15: Forehead

### Exercise Description

- Assume your desired relaxation position, close your eyes, and tune into your exhalations for a few breaths. As you exhale, r-e-l-a-x and r-e-l-a-x and r-e-l-a-x.
- For several exhalations, check your jaws to be sure they are resting comfortably.
- Focus your attention on your nose, cheeks, and eyes for several breaths, relaxing those muscles as you exhale and r-e-l-a-x and r-e-l-a-x as you exhale.
- Now turn your attention to your forehead. Raise only your forehead muscles upward to create muscular tension (Figure 9-5).
- As you exhale, slowly let the tension go and focus on the relaxation that develops in your forehead. Feel, sense, and experience the relaxation in your forehead and your entire face for two to three minutes.
- When ready, flex-stretch-inhale and open your eyes.
- Record your sensations in the Practice Schedule Chart.

### Practice Schedule Chart
### Exercise 15: Forehead

Goal:  To develop the feelings of muscle tension and relaxation in the forehead during each of three sessions.

| Session | Date Performed | Exercise Time | Evaluation |
|---------|----------------|---------------|------------|
| 1 |  |  |  |
| 2 |  |  |  |
| 3 |  |  |  |

Total time spent on this exercise: _____

FIGURE 9-5
*Progressive Relaxation of the Forehead*

### Exercise 16: Basic Relaxation Sequence

Exercise Description
- Assume your desired relaxation position and close your eyes.
- Tune into your exhalation phase of breathing and listen to yourself breathe for several breaths and r-e-l-a-x as you exhale and r-e-l-a-x as you exhale.
- Focus your attention on the supporting environment. Allow the supporting environment to support your body as you exhale and sink into that environment.
- Check your jaw to be sure that it is not clenched but resting comfortably.
- Focus on each of the body parts in sequence—right arm, left arm, shoulder blades and lower neck, mouth, cheeks, eyes, forehead, and entire face—for six to eight exhalations. Eliminate all tension during this session and focus only on the relaxation developing in each body area.
- When ready, flex-stretch-inhale and open your eyes.
- Record your sensations in the Practice Schedule Chart.

Practice Schedule Chart
Exercise 16: Basic Relaxation Sequence

Goal:   To experience muscle relaxation as you perform the basic progressive sequence during each of three sessions.

| Session | Date Performed | Exercise Time | Evaluation |
|---------|----------------|---------------|------------|
| 1       |                |               |            |
| 2       |                |               |            |
| 3       |                |               |            |

Total time spent on this exercise: _____

**Additional Information**

If you are not experiencing relaxation, check the following points. If any of
them apply, make adjustments and try the exercises again:

1. Check your position. Is your body well aligned? Is the supporting
   surface providing maximum support of your muscles?
2. Are you approaching the exercise and the practice session with a
   passive attitude?
3. Are you allowing sensations to occur, or are you trying to force them?
4. Are you allowing sufficient time during each exercise for sensations to
   occur?
5. Are you in an environment that is relatively free of distractions and
   interruptions?
6. Have you practiced the skill as much as the description suggests?
   Perhaps all that is needed is more time and patience.
7. Have you followed the suggested sequence for each exercise?

**USING THE PROGRESSIVE TECHNIQUE
TO ELICIT TOTAL BODY RELAXATION**

You have been learning the basic skills you need to elicit total body relaxation. Now review the preliminary steps that you should go through each time
you perform an exercise:

1. Find the best relaxation position for *you*.
2. Close your eyes and listen to yourself breathe for three or four breaths.
3. Check the supporting environment and allow that environment to do all of the supporting during several breaths.
4. Check for muscular tension anywhere in your body. Are your jaws relaxed, shoulders lowered, eyes and forehead not squinting? Focus on each body part for several breaths as you exhale and relax that part. Do not force relaxation; simply allow it to occur.
5. Begin the relaxation exercise.

During the next several sessions, passively listen to yourself as you silently repeat these steps and progress through them. Eventually, these basic steps will become automatic, and you will not even think about them.

The routine outlined in the preceding pages has been found to be effective in eliciting total body relaxation. Try to get three practice-session routines in during each of the next few days. Remember: This is a progressive relaxation exercise designed to elicit total body relaxation. Following the preliminaries, you begin at your feet and move upward, focusing on the various muscle groups. Eventually you focus on the relaxation that has developed throughout your entire body. Do not be concerned about missing a body part or straying from the sequence. Simply continue as best you can. If you find your thoughts straying, if you experience drifting and floating sensations, or if you are interrupted by distracting sounds, passively disregard them and return to the sequence. If any of the sensations are unpleasant to you, flex-stretch-inhale and begin again. Remember, you are in control at all times. You can start or stop a skill any time you like.

## Exercise 17: Total Relaxation

This exercise is intended to help you eliminate all tension so that you can focus on muscular relaxation. Follow the exercise description while remembering that eventually you are going to develop your own routines.

### Exercise Description

- Assume your desired relaxation position and close your eyes.
- Tune into the exhalation phase of your breathing for several breaths. Listen to yourself breathe and feel the warmth of the air as it passes through your nose.
- Mentally picture the supporting environment. Beginning with your feet and moving upward, focus your attention on each body part that

is in contact with the supporting environment (heels, calves, buttocks, back, shoulders, back of head, elbows, forearms, and hands).

- For two or three exhalations, picture one body part blending with the supporting environment and let that body part be totally supported by the environment.
- As you exhale, silently repeat or think, "I am becoming more and more relaxed with each exhalation."
- In sequence, focus your attention on each of the following body parts, and feel the relaxation develop as you exhale and relax that body part or area: right big toe, right toes, right ankle, right calf, right knee, right thigh, left big toe, left toes, left ankle, left calf, left knee, left thigh, both legs, buttocks, lower back, shoulders and neck, mouth and cheeks, eyes, forehead, right elbow, right forearm, right wrist, right thumb, right index finger, right middle finger, right ring finger, right little finger, entire right arm, left elbow, left forearm, left wrist, left thumb, left index finger, left middle finger, left ring finger, left little finger, entire left arm, both arms.
- Focus on your entire body. Feel and experience the relaxation.
- When ready, flex-stretch-inhale and open your eyes.
- Record your sensations in the Practice Schedule Chart.

Practice Schedule Chart
Exercise 17: Total Relaxation

Goal:　To use progressive relaxation skills to elicit total body relaxation during each of three sessions.

| Session | Date Performed | Exercise Time | Evaluation |
|---------|----------------|---------------|------------|
| 1 | | | |
| 2 | | | |
| 3 | | | |

Total time spent on this exercise: _____

## Additional Information

The total relaxation routine will take about fifteen or twenty minutes. If you sit up immediately after completing the exercise, light-headedness may occur. To avoid this, remain in the relaxed position for several more breaths after you open your eyes. Take another deep inhalation and then slowly return to an upright position.

With practice, you will experience deeper and deeper total body relaxation. The deeper relaxation may leave you with a drowsy, tired feeling. This is caused by the physiological changes that are part of the relaxation response. As body metabolism and oxygen consumption increase, you will notice physical and psychological well-being. Move around a little after the exercise and get the blood flowing to alleviate the tired feeling. If you are still tired and feel like sleeping, then you should listen to your body and sleep. Remember: relaxation is not a substitute for sleep. If you are tired and need sleep, by all means sleep.

## Exercise 18: Individual Exercise

### Exercise Description

- Review Exercise 17, noting especially all of the muscle groups listed in the sequence.
- When developing your individual progressive exercise, you will need to think about which muscle groups you want to include. For example, the right foot versus each toe, arch, ankle, and heel. Be sure to include muscle groups that you have assessed as being more tense than others.
- Determine whether you want to begin your sequence with the feet and move up to the head, or if you want to begin with the head and move down.
- You also need to determine how many exhalations (1, 2, 3 or more) will be spent on each area.
- Once muscle groups and direction have been established, review the five preliminary steps presented earlier. Go through the first four steps before you perform your individual exercise (the fifth step).
- This exercise should be done when you do not have to worry about time, so that you can focus on feeling, sensing, and experiencing the deep relaxation.
- Record your sequence and how you perceived it on the Practice Schedule Chart.

Practice Schedule Chart

Exercise 18: Individual Exercise

Goal: To develop your own progressive relaxation exercise to elicit total body relaxation during each of three sessions.

| Session | Date Performed | Exercise Time | Evaluation |
|---------|----------------|---------------|------------|
| 1 | | | |
| 2 | | | |
| 3 | | | |

Total time spent on this exercise: _____

## SUMMARY

One technique for inducing total body relaxation is progressive relaxation. Progressive relaxation is an attempt by the participant to develop "muscle sense," first by creating muscular tension and then by feeling and experiencing relaxation in the various muscle groups of the body. After muscle sense is developed, only the relaxation phase is used. As muscles become more and more relaxed, impulses to the cortex are slowed, quieting the mind and allowing relaxation to occur.

Exercises involving the muscles of the right and left arm, mouth and cheeks, eyes, forehead, and the basic sequence, when practiced regularly, can induce relaxation. Body position, attitude, time pressures, distractions, and practice are all factors that determine how successful a person is in using progressive relaxation.

When the basic sequence has been learned, you are ready to use progressive relaxation to elicit total body relaxation. Each person can develop a sequence suited to individual preferences. Practiced regularily, progressive relaxation exercises can lead to deep relaxation. It is important to end the relaxation slowly, pausing for a few minutes before standing up and getting blood circulating adequately before resuming normal activity.

## Notes

1 Edmund Jacobson, *You Must Relax* (New York: McGraw-Hill, 1970), p. 154.

2 Ibid., p. 161.

## References

Bernstein, Douglas A., and Borkovec, Thomas D. *Progressive Relaxation Training: A Manual for the Helping Professions.* Champaign: Research Press, 1973.

Jacobson, Edmund. *You Must Relax.* New York: McGraw-Hill, 1970.

Jacobson, Edmund. *Progressive Relaxation.* Chicago: University of Chicago Press, 1938.

Rathbone, Josephine L. *Relaxation.* Philadelphia: Lea and Febiger, 1969.

Rosen, Gerald. *The Relaxation Book: An Illustrated Self-Help Program.* Englewood Cliffs, N. J.: Prentice-Hall, 1977.

Walker, C. Eugene. *Learn to Relax: Thirteen Ways to Reduce Tension.* Englewood Cliffs, N. J.: Prentice-Hall, 1975.

# 10

![black bar]

# TOTAL BODY RELAXATION: SELECTED EXERCISES

Each relaxation instructor develops a particular style that he or she finds most successful in guiding others into a relaxed state. In this chapter, some relaxation exercises that have been used successfully to elicit deep relaxation states are presented.

The first two exercises are presented in detail and in the same format as that used in previous chapters. This consistent use of one format should make it easier for you to learn relaxation skills. Once you have experienced deep relaxation, you will be more aware of the feelings and sensations that are part of that experience. Those feelings and sensations can then be evoked by other exercises, including the last four in this chapter. Individual exercises can be combined, as is done in Exercises 20 (Progressive Relaxation with Benson's method) and 21 (Deepening Relaxation).

Record your practice sessions for Benson's method and for combining Progressive Relaxation with Benson on the practice schedule charts. This will help you to be aware of feelings and sensations when you perform other exercises. As you try the other exercises, you can mentally note sensations, but you need not record them. Exercises 21 through 24 are provided to give you a variety of exercises to select from. When practicing total body relaxation exercises, these can be substituted for other total body exercises, thus adding spice to your daily routine.

## BENSON'S RELAXATION RESPONSE

Benson's relaxation response method was developed and popularized by Herbert Benson, a cardiologist who specializes in hypertension. Dr. Benson is an associate professor of medicine at the Harvard Medical School and director of the Hypertension Section of Beth Israel Hospital in Boston. Components of Benson's method are rooted in transcendental meditation and in many major religions of the world, as well as in many secular writings. Benson has captured the basic components found in all of these writings and reduced them to a simple technique that elicits the relaxation response. His technique is not an attempt to explain meditation or prayer scientifically or to make them mechanical occurrences. Rather, it is an attempt to do what religious leaders have suggested for centuries—to use daily meditation and reflection for the benefit of mind, body, and soul.

The four components presented by Benson are:

1. A Quiet Environment: While learning to elicit the response, you need a quiet, calm environment where you can be alone for the duration of the exercise. Interruptions or background noise can, in the beginning, change your focus and prevent relaxation. A bedroom seems to be the best place in the home. At work, a private office or a conference room may be adequate. You may want to invest in a "Do Not Disturb" sign to hang on the door. (Even the bathroom can serve as your quiet place, especially if it is the only room in which you can be sure you won't be disturbed.)

2. A Mental Device: A relaxation state may be difficult to elicit because your mind is so busy with thoughts about daily activities. Repetition of a single-syllable word, in time with your exhalations, helps you to focus away from thoughts that are distracting and perhaps stressful. The word should be repeated silently or in a low, soothing tone. Some people prefer to picture a word or an object, and some gaze at an object—a flower or a stone. Traditionally, many different words, or "mantras," have been used. Because of its simplicity, follow Benson's suggestion and use the word "one."

3. A Passive Attitude: The opposite of stress and tension is relaxation. Unlike stress and tension, which can be generated within the body, relaxation cannot be forced to occur. Relaxation is a state that you can only allow to happen. Once you have learned the sequence of the

technique, there is no need to be concerned about whether or not relaxation is happening. The harder you work at making it happen, the less likely you are to relax. If your focus on the mental device is interrupted by sounds or people, or if your thoughts wander, passively disregard them. Just return to focusing on your exhalations and your mental device.[1]

4. A Comfortable Position: This method can be learned in any of the basic positions described in Chapter 5. Your body needs to be comfortable and well supported, so that muscle tension is reduced as much as possible. If you find yourself drifting into sleep from a lying position, use a sitting position. Remove or loosen any tight-fitting clothes.

In Chapter 9 you learned how progressive relaxation exercises can elicit relaxation by reducing muscular tension and slowing neural impulses to the higher brain centers was described. As stimulation of the higher brain centers is reduced, there are fewer impulses stimulating muscular tension. The result is total body relaxation.

Benson's method also elicits total body relaxation, but uses a different approach. Benson's method uses a mental device to free the mind from the influence of external stimuli. As the number of stimuli to the cortex is reduced, there is a generalized decrease in sympathetic nervous system activity. This decrease results in decreased oxygen consumption and carbon dioxide elimination, slower heart and respiratory rates, and reduced muscle tension. Reduced muscle tension slows neural impulses to the brain so total body relaxation occurs. Elicitation of the response twice daily, for ten to twenty minutes, brings about a state of physical and mental well-being that has been shown to last well beyond the actual time in relaxation.

Caution: Before you begin to learn how to elicit the response, you should consult with your physician. This is especially true if you have diabetes, high blood pressure, or any condition that requires the regular use of medication for control, or if you are taking medication to relieve depression. Elicitation of the relaxation response alters physiological processes, as do some medications. It is important not to create a risky situation by altering the physiology too much. If you are using any medication, you should check with your doctor before using this technique.

### Exercise 19: Benson's Method

The purpose of Benson's method is to have the participant experience total body relaxation and the resulting physical and mental well-being. Each person can select the position, mental device, and combination of exercises that seem to best meet individual needs.

The preliminary steps for Benson's method are described in Chapter 9. Read the exercise description several times, until you are familiar with the routine and know how and when the mental device is incorporated into the exercise. Perform this exercise during three separate ten-minute practice sessions, and record your sensations in the Practice Schedule Chart.

#### Exercise Description

- Assume the desired relaxation position and close your eyes.
- Tune into your exhalation phase of breathing, listen to yourself breathe for several breaths, and r-e-l-a-x as you exhale, and r-e-l-a-x as you exhale.
- Focus your attention on the supporting environment. Feel, sense, and experience that support as you exhale and allow your entire body to be totally supported by the environment.
- Beginning at the feet, slowly perform a body search looking for any part of your body that is under more tension than the rest (jaws, cheeks, forehead and so on). As you perceive this body part, tune into it for several breaths, and relax that part as you exhale.
- As you continue to exhale through your nose, silently think or repeat the word "one" for five to ten minutes. If you become distracted or find your thoughts wandering, passively disregard this and return, first to your exhalations and then to the word "one."
- When you are ready to end this relaxation, stretch, flex, inhale, and open your eyes.
- Spot a familiar object with your eyes, inhale once again, and slowly sit up.
- After a few more breaths, feel the mental and physical well-being throughout your entire body.
- Record your results on the Practice Schedule Chart.

Practice Schedule Chart

Exercise 19: Benson's Method

Goal:    To elicit the relaxation response during each of three practice sessions.

| Session | Date Performed | Exercise Time | Evaluation |
|---------|----------------|---------------|------------|
| 1 | | | |
| 2 | | | |
| 3 | | | |

Total time spent on this exercise: _____

**Additional Information**

Individuals differ in their abilities to elicit the response. If you are having difficulty, check the following points:

1. Benson suggests not eliciting the response within two hours after eating a meal. Try to schedule this exercise before mealtime.

2. When scheduling the exercise, consider your work schedule and daily routine. You may want to try various times—before breakfast or after you get home from work, for example—to determine what is best for you.

3. After you have used the word "one" for two practice sessions, you may want to use a word that seems more pleasant to you—perhaps "peace," "tranquility," or "serenity." Whatever word or sound you use, prolong the sound of the last syllable until the end of the exhalation.

When you have learned to successfully elicit the relaxation response, try to lengthen your relaxation time to fifteen or twenty minutes for each session.

## Exercise 20: Progressive and Benson's Methods

### Exercise Description
- Assume the desired relaxation position and close your eyes.
- Tune into your exhalations, listen to yourself breathe for several breaths, and r-e-l-a-x as you exhale, and r-e-l-a-x as you exhale.
- Focus on the supporting environment. Allow that environment to support your entire body, and allow yourself to become a part of that surface.
- Beginning with your feet, focus on each of the following body parts for two or three exhalations allowing the part and muscles to relax as you progress: right foot, right ankle, right calf, right knee, right thigh, left foot, left ankle, left calf, left knee, left thigh, the buttocks, the torso area, right hand, right forearm, right shoulder, left hand, left forearm, left shoulder, lower neck muscles, and facial muscles.
- Permit the relaxation that is developing in these areas to generate relaxation throughout the entire body as you exhale and relax for several more breaths.
- As you continue to exhale through your nose, silently think or repeat the word "one" in harmony with each exhalation (or you may use the word or phrase of your choice from now on when doing Benson's method). Continue repeating or thinking your mental device for several minutes.
- Should you become distracted or find your thoughts wandering, passively disregard them and return first to your exhalation and then to your word or phrase.
- When ready to cease relaxation, stretch, flex, inhale, and open your eyes.
- Remain in your relaxation position until you can spot a familiar object, inhale again, stand, and stretch.
- Record your feelings during the relaxation on the Practice Schedule Chart, and then return to your normal daily activities feeling more relaxed.

Practice Schedule Chart

Exercise 20: Progressive and Benson's Methods

Goal:   To elicit the relaxation response during each of three practice
sessions.

| Session | Date Performed | Exercise Time | Evaluation |
|---------|----------------|---------------|------------|
| 1       |                |               |            |
| 2       |                |               |            |
| 3       |                |               |            |

Total time spent on this exercise: _____

## Additional Information

Do not be concerned about missing a body part or the proper sequence. The
sequence is presented only as a guide to help you elicit the relaxation response. It is possible that you will not get as far as the word or phrase you
have chosen before you achieve an altered state of consciousness. If you
become aware of drifting, floating, wandering thoughts, or some other pleasant feeling, passively disregard that and return to where you left off. If you
cannot remember where you were, choose a starting point and simply begin.
The key point is to avoid becoming anxious about where you were or what
you were feeling. If at any time during the relaxation exercise you are uncomfortable about the feelings or sensations you are experiencing, remember that
you are in control and can stop the exercise by flexing, stretching, inhaling,
and opening your eyes.

## SELECTED RELAXATION EXERCISES

You have now been introduced to the basic relaxation techniques. Try these
and make adjustments, alterations, additions, or deletions whenever and
wherever necessary. Remember, though, that some exercises don't work for
everybody. Each of us is unique in how we elicit the relaxation response. And
so included here are some additional techniques that you may find interesting
and helpful.

Try each of these exercises two or three times before making an assessment about its effectiveness for you. You may decide to start each of these exercises by following the preliminary steps suggested in the foundation chapters—choosing a comfortable position, allowing your body to be totally supported by the supporting environment, focusing on exhalations, making a quick body search for tenseness, and exhaling it away, or you may decide to just perform each exercise as described. Be flexible in your effort, but do read each exercise description enough times to be familiar with the content. It is not important if you cannot recall the entire routine. Enjoy whatever relaxation comes from what you are doing. It is important that you approach each exercise with a passive attitude. Remember, you cannot force relaxation to occur; you can only allow it to happen.

When you have mastered the basic skills and tried the selected exercises, try developing your own exercises, using what you have discovered is best for you. There can be as many relaxation exercises as your imagination can create. If you want to look for additional ideas on developing skills and moving beyond the basics, consult *Biofeedback: Your Body at Its Best* by Beata Jencks. You will find this a helpful resource as you try to learn more about evoking altered states of consciousness.

### Exercise 21: Deepening Relaxation[2]

Go ahead and sit or lie down comfortably, hands resting either comfortably by your side or in your lap. Fix your eyes on an object in front of you, above the level of your eyes, and, whenever you wish, go ahead and close them. And now, make a fist with both hands, tighter, *tighter*, as tight as you can and hold it. And now, take a deep breath, hold it, *hold it*, feel the tension in both your arms and your chest. And when you are ready, just allow breath and tension to release at the same time, and allow the relaxation to come upon you. Now, move down to your toes, relax your toes. Relax them. Let them feel very comfortable and relaxed. . . . Allow that relaxation to flow up into the ball of the foot, relaxing it. And now allow the relaxation to flow into the arch of the foot, relaxing it, allowing it to feel comfortable and good. And now allow that relaxation to flow into the heel of the foot, relaxing it, relaxing it; both feet feeling very relaxed, very comfortable, and very good. And now the relaxation flows up into the ankles, relaxing the ankles. And now allow that relaxation to flow into the calves, relaxing the calves, letting them feel comfortable and good. And now let that relaxation flow into the knees, relaxing the knees, letting them feel very comfortable, very relaxed. And now let that relaxation flow into the thighs, relaxing the thighs, letting them feel very comfortable and good. And now let the relaxation flow up into the hips, relaxing the hips, allowing them to feel very comfortable, very good and relaxed. And now let that relaxation flow up into the small of the back, relaxing it, allowing it to feel very comfortable, very relaxed. And now let that relaxation flow up the spine, relaxing the spine. Now allow that relaxation to flow into the shoulders, relaxing the shoulders, letting them feel very comfortable and very relaxed and good. Now let that relaxation flow down into the arms, allowing the arms to relax, letting them feel very comfortable and very good. And now let the relaxation flow into the hands and fingers, just relaxing them, allowing them to relax and feel comfortable. And now allow the relaxation to flow up into the neck, relaxing the neck, letting it feel very comfortable, very good, and very relaxed. And now let it flow up into the scalp, relaxing the scalp, allowing it to feel very comfortable, very relaxed. And now the relaxation is flowing down to the forehead, relaxing the forehead, letting it feel very comfortable, very relaxed. And now allow the relaxation to flow into the eyelids, relaxing the eyelids, allowing them to feel very comfortable, very heavy and relaxed. And if you have not already closed your eyes, just allow your eyes to close and to relax, feeling very comfortable and very relaxed and good. And now let that relaxation flow down into the cheeks and the jaw, relaxing the jaw, relaxing it. And now, taking a deep breath and exhaling through parted lips, feel the relaxation throughout your whole body, just relax even more, relax and feel comfortable. (Pause) With each breath you exhale, just allow yourself to relax even more, relaxing with each exhalation that you make, relaxing even more, and I'll return in a few moments to you. Remember, with each exhalation, just allow yourself to relax even more and move to a more relaxed, comfortable place. (Pause) Relaxing and feeling more comfortable. (Pause) And now, just simply *stretch* and *take a deep breath.* And when you're ready, within the next half minute, return to your normal awake state, feeling very good and very refreshed. Stretch and take a deep breath, and return to your normal awake state.

### Exercise 22: Relaxation Training[3]

Allow yourself at least one-half hour for the session. Select a quiet room with a couch or bed in which you will not be disturbed. Loosen any tight-fitting clothing. Until you learn the procedure, you will want to sit up with the book in your lap so that you can read each step as you proceed; after you become familiar with the method you may wish to go through the entire session lying down on the bed or couch with your eyes closed. The method is called progressive relaxation because it progressively relaxes the body in a step-by-step procedure, beginning with the hands, then moving up the arms to the head, then moving down the body to the feet.

*Step 1.* Clench your right fist and feel the tension sensations in your arm. Clench your fist even tighter, noticing the tightness and the tension in your arm muscles. Now, completely relax your arm, letting your fingers partially straighten out. Observe the difference in the way your arm muscle feels.

*Step 2.* Repeat Step 1, only clench your fist slowly and release it slowly until it is completely relaxed. Pay attention to the difference in the way your arm muscles feel when tensed or relaxed.

*Step 3.* Clench your left fist while keeping the rest of your body as relaxed as possible. Feel the tension sensations in your left arm. Clench your fist tighter, and then completely relax. Notice the difference in the way your arm muscle feels.

*Step 4.* Repeat Step 3 more slowly; then completely relax.

*Step 5.* Bend both arms at the elbows and tense your biceps—the muscles in the front part of your upper arms. Imagine that you are lifting a heavy weight toward your chin. Notice the tension in your biceps. Tense them tighter, and then relax them completely, letting your arms straighten out. Feel the difference between being tense and relaxed.

*Step 6.* Repeat Step 5 more slowly.

*Step 7.* Straighten both of your arms, pressing the backs of your hands down against your legs until you feel the tension in the backs of your arms. Now relax and notice the difference.

*Step 8.* Let your arms completely relax. Lay them at your sides. Search for any tension sensations in your arms and relax them for about a minute. Just let your arms go completely limp. Imagine that the tension is flowing down your arms and out your fingers, leaving your arms completely inactive, limp, and heavy.

*Step 9.* Wrinkle your forehead by raising up your eyebrows as high as you can. Feel the tension throughout your forehead. Then relax your forehead; notice how it smoothes out.

*Step 10.* Frown hard, feeling the tension between your eyes. Now, relax and feel the difference.

*Step 11.* Close your eyelids tightly. Notice the tension all over your eyelids and around your eyes. Relax, but keep your eyes closed.

*Step 12.* Firmly clench your teeth, closing your jaws tightly. Feel the tension sensations in your lower jaw and temples. Now, relax and let your lips part; let your jaw hang loose.

*Step 13.* Press your head back, feeling the tension in your neck. Turn your head left, then right, noticing the different tensions in the sides of your neck. Bend your chin toward your chest. Now let your neck completely relax.

*Step 14.* Shrug your shoulders. Feel the tension in the tops of your shoulders and the sides of your neck. Relax and notice the difference in the way the muscles feel.

*Step 15.* Let your shoulders go completely relaxed, and then your arms, neck, jaws, eyelids, and forehead. Imagine the tensions from these areas flowing out, down your arms and out your fingers. Be limp and loose. Notice the absence of tension sensations in these areas.

*Step 16.* Inhale deeply, and notice the tension in your chest. Hold your breath and observe the sensations of tightness in your muscles. Now relax completely by exhaling.

*Step 17.* Breathe slowly and regularly, letting the air go out of your lungs when you relax. Do this while relaxing the rest of your body.

*Step 18.* Tighten your stomach muscles and keep them tight. Notice the tension in your abdomen. Relax and notice the difference.

*Step 19.* Arch your back, feeling the tension sensations on both sides of your spine. Relax everywhere except in this part of your spine. Now relax your back as well.

*Step 20.* Breathe regularly while relaxing your arms, head, neck, upper and lower torso. Relax any areas in which you feel tension sensations. Let these areas be loose and inactive.

*Step 21.* Straighten your legs and press your heels down hard against the floor or bed. Feel the tension in your thighs and buttocks. Now relax and feel the difference.

*Step 22.* Keep your legs straight and point your toes by moving your feet away from your face. Notice the tension in the calves of your legs. Relax, letting your feet move back to a normal position.

*Step 23.* Move your feet in the opposite direction, back toward your face. Notice the tension in your shins at the front of your lower legs. Relax the muscles in your shins and calves, letting your feet be limp and loose.

*Step 24.* Relax your feet, legs, lower torso, upper torso, arms and hands, neck, jaws, and face. Relax everywhere, feeling no tension. Breathe slowly and deeply, imagining all tensions to flow down your body and out your toes, leaving your body inactive, limp, and heavy. Remain totally inactive for a few minutes.

Any of the steps in this sequence can be isolated and more fully explored and repeated in further sessions. Doing this will enable you to detect very small tensions in your muscles. The more aware you become of your muscle sensations, the easier it will be for you to relax. Your training might be helped by putting the steps of the procedure on tape so that you can follow them without interruption. You can also extend the training by following the steps while sitting or standing. This will help you gain further control over your ability to relax while in public.

Deep muscle relaxation is something you learn how to do by practicing. The progressive relaxation procedure outlined here, with practice, will increase your awareness of and your ability to control nervous tension. But even the first time you try it, you will feel more relaxed.

## Exercise 23: Sense Relaxation Below Your Mind[4]

After reading the following instructions take your time and carry them out.

Sit straight, not rigid, in a chair. Close your eyes and follow your thoughts for one minute. Then let the words go and become aware of how you feel, not how you think you feel or how you'd like to feel but your actual feelings and sensations as they are in the next minute. Now shift your attention to your feet and without moving them in any way become conscious of what they are resting on. Then take fifteen to twenty seconds to feel-experience (rather than think or imagine) the following areas of your body: your feet, each of your toes (without moving them), the top of your feet, your ankles, calves, knees, thighs, buttocks, the chair that is supporting you; your stomach, chest, back, the back of the chair; your shoulders, arms, elbows, forearms, wrists, hands, each of the fingers; your neck, lips, cheeks, nose, eyes, face; forehead, top of the head, back of your head: your entire body. Experience your breathing, the sounds in the room and how you feel right now and then slowly open your eyes. Now with your eyes open, bend your fingers at the joints and begin tapping the top of your head: a lively half-inch bouncing vigorous tap like rain falling (tap fifteen to twenty seconds in each area). Next tap around the ears and the sides of the head. Then over the forehead. Now retap over your entire head, doing an especially good job over any place that feels like it needs a little extra; gradually let the tapping subside. Put your hands down to your sides, close your eyes and become aware of how your head feels as a result of what you've just done and then slowly open your eyes. Now close your eyes and slowly bring your hands toward your face; the heels of your hands come to rest on the cheeks, the palms cover the eyes, the fingers rest over the forehead.

Stay with your eyes covered for one minute; be sensitive to your eyes and the inside of your head; feel how things are there; without creating any changes, just allow whatever wants to occur. Slowly take your hands away, experience how you feel, and open your eyes.

## Exercise 24: Bezzola's Autoanalysis[5]

This method to relieve nervous tension was first described by Bezzola in Switzerland more than half a century ago. The body serves in the procedure as a perfect biofeedback instrument. Beata Jencks found this the most potent method for counteracting extreme nervousness. The procedure is simple.

Sit or lie down comfortably, close the eyes, and pay attention passively to anything which goes on in the body. Put into audible words whatever happens. Do not analyze, do not intellectualize, but just pay attention and report what is sensed. Scan the body and feel more clearly what is happening in different places. For example, "Pressure in the stomach; eyes fluttering; right ear rings; throat tight; left foot itches." Omit all unnecessary words and all references to yourself such as "I" or "my." Just observe and verbalize the location and the sensations felt. Such attending brings gradually a quieting of spontaneous restlessness and a clearing of the mind.

After a few minutes, sensations become fewer and a calm state, possibly sleep, follows. This simple exercise may be used as a treatment procedure by therapists, as a regular prophylactic rest period for overstressed professionals, or as an emergency tool for handling extreme nervousness. If the trainee has learned the method and is sure of his skills of relaxing with exhalations, he may combine the two.

## SUMMARY

There are many techniques available for eliciting total body relaxation. Having a number of techniques in your repertoire provides variation and allows you to determine which techniques work best for you.

Benson's relaxation response method includes four basic components for inducing total body relaxation. The components are (1) a quiet environment, (2) a comfortable position, (3) a mental device, and (4) a passive attitude. These are applicable not only to this method but to most other relaxation techniques. Combining progressive relaxation with Benson's method is an excellent way to deepen relaxation. If total body relaxation is not elicited, you may need to change the mental device you use or the time of day when you use this technique.

The selected exercises developed by Krenz, Holland and Tarlow, Gunther, and Jencks also elicit total body relaxation and provide variety. It is important, with all relaxation exercises, to practice and to make the proper adjustments, alterations, additions, or deletions to meet your individual needs. Most important, however, is to allow relaxation to occur and to enjoy the feelings that result as you learn to elicit total body relaxation.

## Notes

1  Herbert Benson, *The Relaxation Response* (New York: Avon, 1975), pp. 159–162.

2  Eric Krenz, "Deepening Relaxation" (paper distributed at the University of Utah, Salt Lake City, 1980).

3  M. K. Holland and G. Tarlow, *Using Psychology: Principles of Behavior and Your Life* (Boston: Little, Brown, 1980), pp. 81–83.

4  Bernard Gunther, *Sense Relaxation Below Your Mind* (New York: Macmillan, 1968), pp. 10–15.

5  Beata Jencks, *Respiration for Relaxation, Invigoration, and Special Accomplishments* (Salt Lake City: Private Printing, 1974), p. 57.

## References

Benson, Herbert. *The Relaxation Response.* Avon Books, 1975.

Gunther, Bernard. *Sense Relaxation Below Your Mind.* New York: Macmillan, 1968.

Holland, M. K., and Tarlow, G. *Using Psychology: Principles of Behavior and Your Life.* Boston: Little, Brown, 1980.

Jencks, Beata. *Respiration for Relaxation, Invigoration, and Special Accomplishments.* Salt Lake City: Private Printing, 1974.

# 11

![black bar]

# THE MIND: FRIEND
# OR FOE?

If you have a fever and your body aches, it is difficult to concentrate enough
even to balance your checkbook. And if you are excited—perhaps in antici-
pation of going to a party or on a trip—you are likely to feel more energetic
than usual. The mind and the body interact continually, and both are active
participants in the stress response and in the relaxation response. Yet this
interrelationship is often overlooked by those in the health professions. A
common complaint about practitioners in the modern health care system is
that many diagnose and treat only one dimension of the patient—usually the
physical dimension. Too often the mental and emotional problems of the
patient are ignored.

In this chapter we look at the mind/body relationship. We examine
the effects of the mind on the body, problems that occur when the mind has
undesirable effects on the body, and ways to use thought processes to increase and improve health and satisfaction with life.

## MIND, BODY, AND HEALTH

Psychosomatic phenomena relate to or result from the interaction and inter-
dependence of mental (or emotional) and physical aspects of the individual.
Psychogenic phenomena originate in the mind or in mental or emotional
conflict. Between 50 percent and 90 percent of the occupied hospital beds in

the United States at any given time are being used by people suffering from symptoms caused by or aggravated by mental stress. Obviously, the mind/body relationship is powerful—perhaps more powerful than most people recognize.

The influence of the psyche on the body can be seen with ulcers—a relatively common health problem that affects a large number of people. A person whose stomach is vulnerable may develop ulcers as a result of excessive mental and emotional conflicts. Thus, if your mind is actively engaged in tension-producing thoughts, such as worry, guilt, hate, rage, or fear, that mental activity can produce a physiological condition in the stomach that results in ulcers. Yet, if used properly and harnessed for beneficial results, the mind is powerful enough to help heal this same condition.[1] The restorative power is as great as the destructive power. When properly harnessed, the mind can be one of our most valuable aids in improving health and well-being.

This is not to suggest that anyone consciously chooses to have ulcers—that is not a conscious decision. It is more than likely a subconscious response to our thought process. Our subconscious mind has, through a procedure not yet understood, recorded all of the thoughts and impulses that have been experienced through the five senses since birth. These experiences are classified, recorded, and filed, and they can be recalled or withdrawn from the subconscious mind.

We cannot entirely control the subconscious mind, but we can determine to a large degree the thoughts and impressions that the subconscious mind receives. Unlike the conscious mind, the subconscious mind works twenty-four hours a day. If an individual constantly elicits from the subconscious mind thoughts of fear, guilt, worry, and other negative impulses, and if thoughts are filled with tension, the body responds as if this tension-produced state really exists. The mind can actually elicit the stress response. On the other hand, if a person thinks pleasant, relaxing, and tranquil thoughts, the body responds as if it were in a relaxed state.

## DEMONSTRATING THE MIND/BODY RELATIONSHIP

Two techniques illustrate the close mind/body relationship and how the body responds to thought processes.

### Chevreul's Pendulum

The first technique is called Chevreul's pendulum. For this technique, you use a pendulum or some similar object, such as a ring tied to a string or a marble glued to a chain. Sit in a chair and grasp the string or chain between your thumb and forefinger. Rest your elbow on your leg or on the arm of the chair, with the pendulum hanging down about ten inches from your hand. Focus your attention on your exhalations until you feel relaxed. Watch the pendulum closely and remain relaxed, but picture the pendulum swinging back and forth, from side to side. Without consciously moving the pendulum, it will, in a matter of ten to thirty seconds, begin moving in this manner. After it is moving in the visualized direction, imagine it swinging freely in a clockwise circle. Again, the pendulum will swing as visualized.

The pendulum will change directions as you visualize the change. This does not happen because you are consciously moving the pendulum. What is actually taking place is an unconscious (subliminal) motor response (movement). The muscles are contracting in the same sequence as if you were consciously moving the pendulum. But what is actually happening is happening on a subconscious level. You are thinking about a movement—and visualizing it—and the subliminal movements cannot be perceived by you except when they are multiplied, which is what the length of chain does. The end of the pendulum is moving enough to be seen. Yet, the hand and fingers may not be moving enough to be seen easily.

## Biofeedback

A second technique to illustrate the mind/body relationship is biofeedback, shown by a simple electromyograph (EMG) biofeedback portable unit.* The EMG biofeedback machine, a small, simple, portable unit, picks up and responds to changes in muscle tension. Changes in muscle tension are reflected in immediate changes in the frequency and intensity of an audible sound (the higher the frequency and the louder the intensity, the greater the tension) or on a small visual graph on the machine.

Electrodes are attached to the subject's forehead to measure the muscular tension in the frontalis muscles of the forehead. Once the subject is relaxed, a baseline (a beginning measurement against which results can be measured) is established with a low-intensity, low-frequency audible sound. The subject is asked to relive an event in which stress or tension was experienced—to visualize the scene and experience the emotions felt. As the subject does this, muscle tension increases. This increase is illustrated audibly by the sound of the EMG machine. The greater the tension, the greater the frequency and intensity of the sound of the machine.

Next, the trainer directs the subject to relive a quiet scene, one in which relaxation, contentment, and peacefulness were experienced. The subject is instructed to visualize this scene. As he or she does so, the EMG records the relaxation of the frontalis muscles and the frequency and intensity of the audible sound falls, indicating muscular relaxation.

The response is similar to that achieved when using Chevreul's pendulum. The subject is not consciously creating tension in the frontalis muscles during the visualization of the stressful scene, nor does the subject consciously relax the frontalis muscles. The body's response to the thoughts takes place unconsciously at a level that is difficult to perceive consciously.

These exercises illustrate the relationship between mind and body. If you are worrying about something, the worry does not affect just the mind and the thinking processes. It affects the body as well, because the body responds as if whatever you are worrying about is actually taking place. The old adage, "Beware of what you fear, for it shall happen," should not be ignored.

Maxwell Maltz, author of the classic book, *Psychocybernetics*,[2] emphasizes a point that is important to remember. Maltz states that the body cannot tell the difference between an imagined experience and a real one. In other words, if you visualize an event or imagine it vividly, it is recorded in the mind and filed away for future reference. It doesn't matter whether the thought is true or untrue. The mind records it as if it were true.

Have you ever been alone in a house at night and thought you heard someone elsewhere in the house? A creak or squeak can catch your attention, get your heart beating faster, actually make you sweat, tremble, and become rigid or speechless. The increased muscular tension is not caused by the squeak or the noise. It is caused by the perception of the noise. If you think someone is lurking in the darkness of another room, your body responds as if someone is. The fact that it may have been your cat, or the wind, or the furnace starting up, doesn't alter the body's response. If the mind perceives things as being true, the body reacts accordingly.

## Hypnosis

Hypnotists disagree on both the definition and the precise nature of hypnosis. Many believe that hypnosis is a special trance state induced by a hypnotist or by the subject. Others believe that a trance is unnecessary, because all the effects that can be produced in a trance can also be produced without the trance. All would agree that hypnosis involves giving suggestions and that it is induced by certain stimuli, such as visual fixation, concentration, repetition, monotonous stimuli, or through relaxation.

Hypnosis can also illustrate the mind/body relationship. Under hypnosis, if subjects sitting in a warm room (65°F) are told they are in a cold room with inadequate clothing, their bodies are likely to begin shivering. If they are told they are in a hot, humid, tropical climate, they may begin to sweat. It has also been reported that subjects developed blisters when they were told that the hypnotist's finger was a hot poker and the hypnotist touched them with that finger. Hypnosis has been used effectively to block out pain during surgery, childbirth, removal of teeth, and severe headaches. It has also been used to remove warts, to stop internal bleeding, and to slow bleeding of certain body parts during surgery. In each of these situations, the mind alters the body's responses.

## SELF-CONCEPT

Are you a slave to your subconscious? Are you nonmechanical? Do you fear heights or water? Are you a "C" student, no matter how hard you try? Are you poor in mathematics? Are you accident prone? We all believe certain things about ourselves, and these form our self-concept—how we feel about ourselves and what we believe we are capable of accomplishing.

Thought patterns can be cyclical. If you begin to think negative thoughts and spend more and more time thinking negatively, these negative thoughts tend to produce more negative thoughts. Eventually, your attitude toward your life and yourself is saturated with negativism. You begin to focus on things that go wrong, and when things do go wrong, your negative attitude becomes a self-fulfilling prophecy. Tension, stress, frustration, and anxiety become a way of life. "Why try, I know I'll fail." Tension mounts and feeds the negative self-concept.

Can this cycle be broken, and, if so, how? It can be, with work, and with help from family, from friends, and perhaps from a therapist. You must be aware of the cycle and want to break it. An emphasis on positive life experiences must replace the emphasis on negative ones. This process can be facilitated by a program of stress management. If you can reduce the stress in your life, you will feel better and will become better able to handle stress; and this can help to improve your self-concept as well as the quality of your life.

## BODY BREATHING EXERCISES

Body-breathing exercises allow you to breathe in and out of the same body part, breathe in and out of different body parts, and even can allow a complete reversal, such as breathing in through the feet and out through the arms. These exercises help relax the body or a particular body part.

Beata Jencks developed an exercise, called the long breath, in which a person breathes in and out of various parts of the body. Body breathing exercises are variations of long-breath exercises. Body breathing exercises help relax muscle groups and remove tensions from various parts of the body. The first exercise here is an adaptation of Jencks' long-breath exercise.[3]

## Exercise 25: The Long Breath

Exercise Description
- Assume a comfortable position, exhale, relax, and sink down into the supporting environment.
- Exhale, relax, and allow your legs (upper legs, lower legs, ankles, feet) to become heavy as they are supported by the environment.
- On the next exhalation, relax, and let the entire trunk, hips, and buttocks sink into the environment. On the next breath, as you exhale, relax the upper arms, forearms, and hands. Exhale, relax, and allow the entire body to be supported by the surrounding environment.
- Now, inhale through the nose. As you exhale, imagine, in a manner in which you are comfortable, the exhaled air flowing out through the bottom of the feet. Following each inhalation, visualize or think about that air flowing down the trunk, the legs, and permit the air to flow out through the feet (either the bottoms of the feet or out the toes). Feel, sense, and experience any sensations.
- Repeat the above sequence on each successive breathing cycle for several cycles.
- After three or four breathing cycles, simultaneously, stretch, flex, inhale deeply, and open the eyes.
- Record the sensations noted on the Practice Schedule Chart.

Practice Schedule Chart
Exercise 25: The Long Breath

Goal:  To perform the long breath exercise during each of three practice
sessions.

| Session | Date Performed | Exercise Time | Evaluation |
|---------|----------------|---------------|------------|
| 1       |                |               |            |
| 2       |                |               |            |
| 3       |                |               |            |

Total time spent on this exercise: _____

## Exercise 26: Body Breathing to Remove Tension or Pain

The basic long-breath exercise can be adapted to body breathing in a variety
of ways. For example, imagine that you have muscular tension or pain in the
low back area. The following adaptation may be useful (preliminary relaxation is condensed for greater simplicity).

Exercise Description

- Assume a comfortable position.
- Exhale, relax, and allow your body to sink down and be supported by
  the surrounding environment.
- Imagine that as you breathe in, the air is flowing into the body
  through the nose. Visualize the air streaming down through the trunk,
  and as you exhale, imagine the air flowing out of the body in the lower
  back area.
- Imagine this same sequence on each successive breath and visualize, in
  any manner you choose, the air carrying the tensions and pains of the
  lower back out of the body. On each breath, the lower back becomes
  more and more relaxed and more and more comfortable.
- When the exercise is completed, flex, stretch, inhale, and open your
  eyes.
- Record any feelings or sensations on the Practice Schedule Chart.

Practice Schedule Chart
Exercise 26: Body Breathing to Remove Tension or Pain

Goal:   To perform the body breathing exercise to remove tension or pain
during each of three practice sessions.

| Session | Date Performed | Exercise Time | Evaluation |
|---------|---------------|---------------|------------|
| 1       |               |               |            |
| 2       |               |               |            |
| 3       |               |               |            |

Total time spent on this exercise: _____

## USING THE MIND IN BENEFICIAL WAYS

Our minds can cause problems in our lives and our health. However, if we
can learn to control our minds, we can enhance health, change attitudes,
bolster self-concept, help eliminate feelings of inferiority, and live more effectively. Basic exercises that use the mind for relaxation involve self-suggestion
during the exhalation phase of the breathing rhythm. When this is coupled
with sensory awareness and supporting environment exercises, a synergistic
effect occurs that compounds the desired effect.

Caution:  These exercises can cause a stressful and unpleasant response
in some people. If this begins to happen to you, just flex, stretch, and
come out of the exercise. *You are in charge.* A person who has been
under or is involved in psychological counseling should not use these
exercises without supervision from a therapist or doctor.

### Exercise 27: Sequential Relaxation Using the Mind

The sequential relaxation exercise using the mind uses components of many
of the exercises learned earlier. It is similar to the sequential relaxation exercises, but is coupled with the mind. Read the exercise several times before
performing it. Record sensations in the Practice Schedule Chart.

Exercise Description

- Assume a comfortable position and focus your attention on the exhalation phase of your breathing rhythm.
- Passively observe your breathing and allow your body to relax, slow down, and sink down on each successive exhalation.
- Simply r-e-l-a-x, and r-e-l-a-x, and r-e-l-a-x as you exhale, and feel your body sinking down into the supporting environment. Allow the environment to accept your body as the tensions leave and you maintain your position with a minimum of muscular tension. Simply r-e-l-a-x, and r-e-l-a-x, and r-e-l-a-x.
- As you become more and more relaxed and comfortable, focus all of your attention on a foot and an ankle.
- As you exhale, feel a comfortable heaviness begin to develop in the foot and ankle. Allow that foot and ankle to sink down as you relax. Imagine that foot and ankle relaxing, spreading out, and blending in with the supporting environment. In any manner that you choose, imagine the tensions flowing out of your foot into the surrounding environment.
- Next, move your attention to the lower leg or calf region of one leg and visualize the muscles relaxing and the tensions flowing out of this area. Feel the pull of gravity on that lower leg and as the leg relaxes, allow it to be supported by the floor through the ankle and foot (sitting position), or allow it to be supported entirely by the environment.
- Repeat the procedure on the other lower leg region.
- Relax, let go, and as you exhale, imagine the tensions flowing out of the muscles. Let go, relax, and allow the environment to totally support your lower leg.
- Now focus your attention on the upper leg or thigh, and relax the muscles as you exhale. Again, imagine in some manner the tensions flowing out of that leg as you exhale. Move your attention to the other upper leg and imagine the tensions flowing out as you exhale, relax, and let go. Both legs are entirely relaxed, and as you continue to exhale, sink down and allow the environment to support you.
- Do the same with the trunk of the body. As you exhale, relax, sink down, and imagine the body becoming soft as the tensions flow out. Allow the environment to support you entirely as you feel, sense, and experience whatever is happening to you.

- Now focus attention on the arms, forearms, and hands. As you exhale, imagine the muscles becoming relaxed. Exhale, relax, and let go and feel the pull of gravity as the arms and hands become comfortably heavy and relaxed.
- Attention should now be focused on the head and neck. As you exhale, imagine all the tensions flowing to the outside of the body in this region. Exhale, relax, and let go.
- At this time, you are relaxed. The tensions within the body have been released. As you exhale, allow the body to be comfortably heavy and relaxed.
- Remain in this relaxed state for several minutes, and enjoy the lack of tension in the body.
- When you have completed the exercise and when ready, simultaneously stretch, flex, take a deep breath, and open the eyes.
- You are now ready to return to your normal activity. Record your sensations on the Practice Schedule Charts.

Practice Schedule Chart
Exercise 27: Sequential Relaxation Using the Mind

Goal:   Perform the sequential relaxation exercise using the mind during each of three practice sessions.

| Session | Date Performed | Exercise Time | Evaluation |
|---------|----------------|---------------|------------|
| 1 | | | |
| 2 | | | |
| 3 | | | |

Total time spent on this exercise: _____

## Exercise 28: Visualization of Relaxed Scenes

Visualization of relaxed scene or returning mentally to recapture a happy, relaxed moment in your life can be an effective technique for relaxing or for preparing yourself for other techniques. When you select a scene, the following criteria are important: (1) It must be a happy scene—a scene that focuses on an enjoyable experience. (2) It must be a scene in which you are relaxed. (3) It should be a scene in which you are inactive.

These criteria are based on the mind/body relationship. If you visualize running a marathon or hiking up a mountain, the subliminal motor movements are taking place. The muscle action sequence is being fired, and this will hinder relaxation. However, if you visualize yourself after the race, sitting, relaxed, contented, fulfilled, and basking in the sunshine, this will assist the relaxation.

Sample scenes that people have discussed in workshops, and that are quite common, include lying in the sun at the beach (maybe visualizing the waves as they roll into shore and then recede); relaxing in a small boat fishing on a comfortably warm day, the sun beating down and the body soaking up its warmth, and the boat lazily rocking in the water; relaxing in a cozy room in front of a fireplace and watching the flames flicker and dance; vacationing at a cottage on a trip. Many people will visualize past experiences rather than creating new scenes.

### Exercise Description

- Close your eyes.
- Visualize a relaxing scene.
- Record your sensations on the Practice Schedule Chart.

### Practice Schedule Chart
### Exercise 28: Visualization of Relaxed Scenes

Goal:   To visualize a relaxing scene and perform the visualization exercise during each of three practice sessions.

| Session | Date Performed | Exercise Time | Evaluation |
|---------|----------------|---------------|------------|
| 1       |                |               |            |
| 2       |                |               |            |
| 3       |                |               |            |

Total time spent on this exercise: _____

## VISUALIZATION FOR STRESS MANAGEMENT

Have you ever had a problem that was always on your mind, one you couldn't shake? Is school constantly on your mind? Do you bring problems from work home with you? Such preoccupation with problems may be necessary and productive at times, but it can become a habit that interferes with your relationships with the people around you and with those you love.

The following exercises are advanced uses of the imagination, and you may have to practice for several weeks before they are useful to you. Enough descriptive information is provided to help you develop your own exercise. You may use the ideas presented, or you may want to adapt those or invent new ideas that fit your situation. Record your evaluations of the exercises in the Practice Schedule Charts.

### Exercise 29: The Clothes Hanger

If you normally change clothes soon after arriving home, this habit can be useful in changing your thinking as you switch environments.

Exercise Description

- As you remove your clothing, article by article, imagine that you are hanging up your problems with the clothes. As you remove a shirt or blouse, say to yourself that this piece of clothing represents the problem of John Doe, for example, and it will remain in the closet this evening. As you do this, visualize old John Doe being hung up on the hanger.
- The pants or skirt can represent a different problem, or one article, such as a coat or sweater, may represent all the problems—all stresses and thoughts from work.
- When you begin this exercise, you will find that thoughts of work continue to enter your mind regularly. Don't worry about this or become frustrated. Each time you catch yourself and realize you are thinking about your job, say, "Return to the hanger where I have put you—I'll take you off when *I'm* ready." Visualize the problems being hung up again.
- If you practice this exercise faithfully, within a week or so you will probably make it through an evening with few thoughts about your job. When this occurs, you have made strides in regaining control of your thought processes.

Practice Schedule Chart

Exercise 29: The Clothes Hanger

Goal:   Perform the clothes hanger exercise during each of three practice
sessions.

| Session | Date Performed | Exercise Time | Evaluation |
|---------|----------------|---------------|------------|
| 1       |                |               |            |
| 2       |                |               |            |
| 3       |                |               |            |

Total time spent on this exercise: _____

## Exercise 30: The Box

Exercise Description

- As you arrive home, imagine that a box with a lid on it is next to the
  door. Before entering, exhale, relax, and imagine all of your thoughts
  of work flowing from your mind into the box and the lid shutting.
  Now you know where the thoughts are.
- Again, if thoughts about your job come into your mind regularly, as
  they probably will at first, exhale and send them back to the box and
  shut the lid. If they persist, imagine a lock on the box and lock in the
  thoughts.
- Don't be frustrated if these thoughts persist. With practice, you will
  notice them diminishing, and eventually you will be able to spend
  evenings, weekends, and vacations free from thoughts of work, if you
  so desire.
- If you must regularly or occasionally bring work home, put it away
  during supper, while playing with the children, or when getting ready
  for sleep. When you are ready to work, imagine the box opening and
  the thoughts coming to you.
- Remain in control—you are the boss of your thoughts.

Practice Schedule Chart
Exercise 30: The Box

Goal:   To perform the box exercise during each of three practice sessions.

| Session | Date Performed | Exercise Time | Evaluation |
|---------|----------------|---------------|------------|
| 1 | | | |
| 2 | | | |
| 3 | | | |

Total time spent on this exercise: _____

## Visualization and Performance

Visualization has been used for decades by athletes and others to upgrade physical performance. A great deal of research has been done on the effectiveness of visualization. Much of the research has found that visualization, or mental practice, is an aid in increasing physical skills, as long as the individual is familiar with the skill to be learned.

Many people have discussed or written about the impact of visualization on performance in areas other than physical skills—for example, on making money, improving job performance, increasing sales, giving speeches, and enhancing self-concept. The evidence indicates that visualization can improve many kinds of performance.

Visualization is effective when used with relaxation skills. The rational mind, which serves as a gatekeeper of conscious thoughts, slows down its conscious thought processes when relaxed. This allows visualizations to be fed into the subconscious mind. Eventually the subconscious mind begins to accept visualizations as experiences. (Remember: The subconscious mind cannot tell the difference between a real experience and an imagined one.) Thus, if you visualize yourself performing effectively in a particular situation, you gradually develop the belief that you can perform effectively in that situation.

## Positive Affirmation Statements—Self-Suggestion

Closely related to visualization and performance is the use of positive affirmation statements as a means of self-suggestion. These statements feed the subconscious mind with positive attitudes about self-concept, health, and other objectives. As with visualization and performance, when such statements are repeated while you are in a relaxed state, they have a more rapid effect on the subconscious mind.

When using positive affirmation statements this way, you first perform any of the relaxation exercises to get in the relaxed state and open the subconscious to suggestion. Once you are relaxed, repeat the statement you have created five or more times in succession. This repetition imprints the thoughts in the subconscious mind. As you continue, feel the positive feelings that accompany the thoughts. To be effective, this process should be repeated two or three times daily. Most people who recommend positive affirmation statements suggest that you use them every morning upon waking, every evening just before going to sleep, and, if possible, several other times each day. The more often the statements are repeated, the more rapid and noticeable the desired effect.

### Developing a Self-Suggestion Exercise

Positive affirmation statements work very effectively when combined with visualization. After achieving a relaxed state, repeat the positive affirmation statements, at least five and perhaps as many as twenty times. Then mentally picture yourself performing what you want to do or looking as you want to look, for example. Picture in your mind's eye exactly what you want to accomplish or be. Try to feel the excitement, the feelings of satisfaction that you will feel when you accomplish the goal you are working toward. After mentally seeing and feeling accomplishment of the goal, repeat the positive affirmation statements, again five to twenty times. Then enjoy the relaxed state for a few minutes before terminating the exercise.

When creating or selecting positive affirmation statements, keep in mind two basic points: (1) All statements should be positive. Focus the statement on what you will be doing—not on what you will not be doing. For example, state "I am relaxed" rather than "I am not tense" or "I am slender" rather than "I am not fat." (2) All statements should be as brief as possible. Focus on thoughts about precisely what you would like to achieve.

Listed here are some positive affirmation statements. It is best, however, if each person creates statements to meet his or her particular needs.

*To enhance self-concept and achieve a positive mental attitude:*

- I succeed because I believe I can.
- Every day in every way, I am better and better.
- I am filled with loving kindness.[4]

- I am at peace with nature—and myself.
- I am happy and content with my job.
- I will succeed.
- Optimism makes me enthusiastic.

*To encourage weight loss:*

- "I am proud of my ideal weight." (Visualize how you look at this weight.)
- I feel pride and joy as I approach my desired weight.
- Every day in every way, I am thinner and thinner.
- I am satisfied; my hunger has been eliminated.
- I desire carrots.

*To foster relaxation, health, and healing:*

- I am relaxed.
- I am healthy, happy, and relaxed.
- My body heals itself.
- Pain free, happy me!
- I am healthy, refreshed, and full of energy.
- I believe.
- I forgive others.
- Silence is soothing and healing.
- "I am in God's healing hands."
- I am physically breathing because I am spiritually healthy.
- "The doctor dresses the wound, God heals it."

*To alleviate worry:*

- I forget the past and the future—I live for the present.
- This will be a great day.
- I accept the challenge; I will eagerly overcome it.

## SUMMARY

The mind has a powerful effect on health, happiness, and success in life. The close relationship that exists between the mind and body can be demonstrated by Chevreul's pendulum, biofeedback, and hypnosis. Each of these illustrates that the mind cannot tell the difference between a real experience and an imagined experience.

The self-concept is also important in the mind/body relationship. The person who learns to reduce the stress in his or her life and to handle stress better is likely to improve his or her self-concept and quality of life.

A variety of exercises can be useful in developing a positive mind/ body relationship. Body breathing exercises—such as the long breath and body breathing to remove tension or pain—are ways to use the mind for beneficial results. Others are sequential relaxation using the mind, visualization of relaxed scenes, and visualization exercises such as the clothes hanger and the box.

Positive affirmation statements can be used as a means of self-suggestion. Such statements feed the subconscious mind with positive thoughts about self-concept, health, and so on. These statements are most effective when used by a person in a relaxed state.

### Notes

1 K. R. Pelletier, *Mind as Healer, Mind as Slayer* (New York: Dell, 1977).

2 Maxwell Maltz, *Psychocybernetics* (New York: Simon & Schuster, 1960), pp. 28–29.

3 Beata Jencks, *Respiration for Relaxation, Invigoration, and Special Accomplishments* (Salt Lake City: Private Printing, 1974), p. 26.

4 C. Norman Shealy, *90 Days to Self-Health* (New York: Dial, 1977), p. 59.

### References

Holland, M. K., and Tarlow, G. *Using Psychology: Principles of Behavior and Your Life.* Boston: Little, Brown, 1980.

Iselin, Walter C. *The Effects of Programmed Relaxation Exercises on the Shooting of Basketball Freethrows.* Master's thesis, University of Wisconsin–La Crosse, 1979.

Jencks, Beata. *Respiration for Relaxation, Invigoration, and Special Accomplishments.* Salt Lake City: Private Printing, 1974.

Jencks, Beata. *Your Body: Biofeedback at its Best.* Chicago: Nelson-Hall Publishers, 1977.

Oxendine, J. B., *Psychology of Motor Learning.* Englewood Cliffs, N. J.: Prentice-Hall, 1968.

Peale, Norman V. *Enthusiasm Makes the Difference.* Englewood Cliffs, N. J. Prentice-Hall, 1967.

Peale, Norman V. *The Power of Positive Thinking.* Englewood Cliffs, N. J.: Prentice-Hall, 1956.

Shealy, C. Norman. *90 Days to Self-Health.* New York: Dial Press, 1977.

Stone, W. Clement. *Success Through a Positive Mental Attitude.* Englewood Cliffs, N. J.: Prentice-Hall, 1960.

Stone, W. Clement. *The Success System That Never Fails*. Englewood Cliffs, N. J.: Prentice-Hall, 1962.

Waitley, D. "Visualize Your Way to Success." *Success Unlimited* 25 (1978): 38–39, 48, 50, 52, 54, 56.

# PART FOUR

![black bar]

# BEYOND THE BASICS

Relaxation is a vital component of a stress management program. However, any program that does not include other areas of stress management would be too narrow. Part Four examines additional components, beyond basic relaxation skills, that are needed in a holistic approach to stress management. Because each individual has different needs, the necessary components for an effective stress management program will vary from person to person. Some of the components that many people find most useful are presented here. When planning and developing your stress management program, you will want to include as many of these components as are valuable to you.

# 12

<br>
**████████████**

# PRACTICAL
# RELAXATION

When most people think of relaxation, they think of sitting in a comfortable chair or lying on a bed, in comfortable clothing, in a quiet room with dim lighting and a soft breeze. These are ideal circumstances, and this environment is a good one for relaxation.

But these are not the ordinary circumstances of daily life. How can you relax when you are under stress? Many people are in stressful environments throughout the day—must they wait until evening to relax? Are there any skills that can be practiced while you are standing, walking, or running? Is it possible to manage stress while working or during an argument? It is possible to manage stress, to relax, in almost any situation. Further, it is important to learn to manage stress when anticipating a stressful situation and when in a stressful environment.

The phrase "practical relaxation skills" refers to a group of exercises designed to be practiced in circumstances not normally used for relaxation. Practical relaxation skills are not necessarily total body relaxation skills and do not usually produce the typical physiological benefits of deep total body relaxation. However, practical relaxation skills are useful in managing and controlling the stress level or stress response. These skills can help you to manage reaction or overreaction to stressors when the stress response is elicited.

## DIFFERENTIAL RELAXATION:
## PRACTICAL SKILLS FOR ROUTINE ACTIVITIES

Differential relaxation skills can be practiced during an ordinary day. There are many stressful situations in which you must be mentally alert and must continue standing, sitting, or walking. At such times total body relaxation is out of the question, although you may want to control stress level and energy expenditure. In such situations, these techniques, or adaptations of them, can be helpful.

Differential relaxation is the relaxation of various muscles while you are active. It involves learning to differentiate between muscle tensions required to perform a particular task and muscle tensions that are not needed for that task. Differential relaxation also involves minimizing the tension level, so that the task is performed with minimal muscle tension.

When learning differential relaxation, you use the same basic techniques used during total body exercises. Learn these skills in nonstressful situations before using them in stressful ones.

### Exercise 31: Sitting While Mentally Alert

Participating in a meeting, being interviewed for a job, talking on the telephone—these and similar situations can be stressful. Such situations require your full attention. Yet you are likely to want, also, to manage the stress level and conserve body energy. The following exercise can be done while in a sitting position. The various muscles of the back and other muscles needed to maintain the sitting position are tense enough to maintain the position, while other muscles not needed are relaxed. While relaxed in this way, you can remain alert.

### Exercise Description

- As you consciously decide to relax in the sitting position, focus on the exhalation phase of the breathing cycle (with the eyes open) for two or three breaths.
- Feel yourself let go, relax, and sink down into the chair. Allow the chair to support you entirely, relax your muscles, and feel the heaviness as the pull of gravity exerts itself on the body.
- Once you feel the heaviness and sinking down sensation, mentally remain in the discussion or meeting as you disregard the body.
- When there is quiet or you feel tension, repeat the exercise for two or three breaths.

- With practice, and when necessary, you can learn to argue, raise your voice, and so on, and yet feel the composure that accompanies self-control and a relaxed feeling.

Record your results in the Practice Schedule Chart.


Practice Schedule Chart
Exercise 31: Sitting While Mentally Alert

Goal:   To perform the sitting while mentally alert exercise during each of three practice sessions.

| Session | Date Performed | Exercise Time | Evaluation |
|---------|----------------|---------------|------------|
| 1 |  |  |  |
| 2 |  |  |  |
| 3 |  |  |  |

Total time spent on this exercise: _____


**Exercise 32: Supporting Environment Exercise While Performing a Task**

While performing a task, focus on what needs to be done and determine which body parts or muscle groups are needed. Arrange your body so that you are in a comfortable position, well aligned, with as much environmental support as possible. As an example, say you are at a desk writing. The wrist, fingers, and lower arm are required for this task. Other body parts can be relaxed. Shift your position so that the feet are flat on the floor, both arms from the elbows on down are resting comfortably on the desk top, and the chair supports the trunk of your body.


Exercise Description

- Exhale . . . relax, and allow the body to sink down and be supported by the supporting environment for two to three breaths.
- Quickly search the body for tension. When tension is located, exhale and relax the tension away.

- As you relax, begin the task using only those muscles needed to perform the task (for example, writing a memo requires only the use of the arm and hand, not clenched jaws).
- Occasionally search your body to keep it in a relaxed, well-supported position.
- Record your use of this exercise in the Practice Schedule Chart.

Practice Schedule Chart
Exercise 32: Supporting Environment Exercise While Performing a Task

Goal:   To perform the supporting environment exercise while performing a task during each of three practice sessions.

| Session | Date Performed | Exercise Time | Evaluation |
|---------|----------------|---------------|------------|
| 1 | | | |
| 2 | | | |
| 3 | | | |

Total time spent on this exercise: _____

## Exercise 33: Supporting Environment Throughout the Day

Exercise Description

- Throughout the entire day, whenever you think of it, quickly search your body for tensions and exhale away unnecessary tensions.
- Then adjust your body so that you have support from the environment. Exhale, relax, sink into the environment, and allow the environment to support your body.

Many participants in workshops report that this exercise is very useful. Throughout the day, when the body is not aligned and there is needless muscle tension, a great deal of energy is wasted. This energy depletion accumulates throughout the day. As a result, many people experience exhaustion late in the day—not from work (although they think it is) but because they used more energy than necessary on many tasks. If you do this exercise periodically throughout the day, you may discover you are more energetic later in the day and can be more effective than usual during those hours.

Practice Schedule Chart

Exercise 33: Supporting Environment Throughout the Day

Goal:   To perform the supporting environment throughout the day exercise during each of three practice sessions.

| Session | Date Performed | Exercise Time | Evaluation |
|---------|----------------|---------------|------------|
| 1       |                |               |            |
| 2       |                |               |            |
| 3       |                |               |            |

Total time spent on this exercise: _____

## DIFFERENTIAL RELAXATION WHEN STANDING AND WALKING

Feelings and sensations of tension can be controlled while you are engaged in total body activities that require varying degrees of tension. The technique used is described in the standing and walking exercises and can be adapted to other activities.

### Exercise 34: Standing

We all spend a lot of time standing. Stress management and energy conservation techniques can be learned and used in the standing position. The basic concept is used in the walking technique that follows. The standing technique is quite similar to "the stand" sensory awareness exercise described earlier.

Exercise Description
- Stand erect with the eyes open and focused at an object or point four to six feet in front of you.
- Exhale, relax, and let go of muscular tensions while you maintain good posture.

- Focus your attention inward (while keeping your eyes open) and feel the pull of gravity and the weight of the body pushing downward to the feet.
- Allow the floor to support the body and its weight via the feet, ankles, lower legs, and upper legs.
- Exhale, relax muscles not needed (abdomen, shoulders, arms, hands), and allow the floor and other body parts to support you with a minimum of muscular tension.
- Repeat this procedure for two to three breaths, then maintain the position for thirty seconds to a minute.

Practice Schedule Chart
Exercise 34: Standing

Goal:   To perform the standing exercise during each of three practice sessions.

| Session | Date Performed | Exercise Time | Evaluation |
|---------|----------------|---------------|------------|
| 1 | | | |
| 2 | | | |
| 3 | | | |

Total time spent on this exercise: _____

## Exercise 35: Walking

You only have to watch a group of people walk to sense the tension level of modern life. Most people walk at a medium to rapid pace. When performing sensory awareness exercises while walking, you will be amazed at the tension level throughout your body—including tension in body parts not needed to perform the simple task of walking. The walking exercise is designed to slow you down, to conserve energy, and to give you a sensation of relaxation and composure. This comes from letting the body walk, rather than making it walk.

When learning to use walking to manage stress and to conserve energy, it is best to use two separate exercises. The first exercise exaggerates

walking while using the exhalation phase of breathing coupled with movement. After that is practiced, the exhalation phase is coupled with a normal
walking pattern.

### Exercise Description 35a (Exaggerated Walking)
- To perform this exercise, focus on the breathing rhythm while in a standing position.
- After three to four breathing cycles, begin to walk slowly as you exhale.
- At the end of the exhalation phase of the breathing cycle, stop and remain standing still until you have completed the inhalation. Then, as you begin exhaling, slowly begin your walking. Walk only in time with the exhalation, do not force it.
- Repeat the procedure until you begin to feel the speed at which the body wants to move.
- Breathe normally as you perform this exercise. *Do not* alter the breathing rhythm but change your walking pattern to fit the breathing cycle.
- Record your use of this exercise in the Practice Schedule Chart.

### Exercise Description 35b (Regular Walking)
- After you begin to feel the pace of walking established by the breathing cycle in the exaggerated walking exercise, walk continuously.
- Consciously focus your attention on the breathing cycle.
- Breathe normally, disregard the inhalation phase, and focus only on the exhalations.
- Allow your walking speed to be dictated by your exhalations.
- While walking, and after a pace is established, relax the arms, shoulders, and hands as you exhale. Continue in a position of good posture with head held upright.
- Occasionally, search the body for unnecessary tensions, and when you locate them, exhale and relax them away.
- Record your use of this exercise on the Practice Schedule Chart.

Many people say that, once the pace is established, they can think of other things while walking. In fact, people who normally rush from place to place report that, when they slow their pace, they are more relaxed, feel more composed, and can use the additional time to prepare for the meeting, class, or other activity toward which they are headed. In addition, the time difference of strolling versus a hurried pace is minimal.

**Variations**   After you have learned the walking exercise, you can use the same procedure for a variety of activities. While jogging, you can adjust your pace to the exhalation phase—and you may find you are less winded and less tired after a long jog.

      When running, the body search can be done. As you exhale, relax the shoulders, hands, fingers, and other body parts not needed to sustain the rapid pace. Over a long distance, a great deal of energy can be saved and used more effectively to maintain the muscle groups needed for running. Also, as you focus your mind inward you can monitor the body. This increased attention can alert you to when the pace can be quickened—or when the pace must be slowed down.

Practice Schedule Chart
Exercise 35(a): Walking (Exaggerated Walking)

Goal:    To perform the exaggerated walking exercise during each of three practice sessions.

| Session | Date Performed | Exercise Time | Evaluation |
|---|---|---|---|
| 1 | | | |
| 2 | | | |
| 3 | | | |

Total time spent on this exercise: _____

Practice Schedule Chart

Exercise 35(b): Walking (Regular Walking)

Goal:   To perform the regular walking exercise during each of three practice sessions.

| Session | Date Performed | Exercise Time | Evaluation |
|---------|----------------|---------------|------------|
| 1 | | | |
| 2 | | | |
| 3 | | | |

Total time spent on this exercise: _____

## RELAXATION WHILE WAITING

Impatience is a stress producer in modern society. It seems as if everyone has more to do and less time to do it all in. This increased work load often creates time pressures. Anything that causes unusual or undesired delays can increase stress. Usually impatience is a self-chosen stressor. By this, we mean that the frustration or anger that occurs when you are waiting are results of perception—of how you perceive the waiting.

If you can do something to eliminate the wait and so remove impatience—do it! There is no sense in allowing a wait to become a stressor if you can reduce or eliminate the wait. If you cannot do anything about it, why worry, get frustrated, or angry? This only elicits the stress response. Accept that the situation is beyond your control and think of this extra time as a gift—a gift of time for reading, beginning a project, thinking, reflecting, or relaxing. All of these activities are more beneficial than becoming impatient, tense, or worried.

When you are forced to wait, use the basic, practical, relaxation skills discussed earlier in this chapter and adapt them to the situation. For example, imagine you are waiting in a line for gas. If you are safely out of the line of traffic, put your car in neutral or in park. Then exhale, relax your body as you exhale, and do the sitting exercise while mentally alert. This is certainly more beneficial than fretting and fuming about having to wait in the gas line. If the car in front of you moves, the drivers behind you are certain to honk their horns to remind you to move up.

## RELAXATION AND SLEEP

Some relaxation principles and techniques can be useful in helping you fall asleep and in achieving relaxed sleep. Josephine Rathbone writes that "the low level of motor activity is the most striking sign of sleep; but sleep does not always bring relaxation, and even deep relaxation can be achieved without sleep. When one learns how to relax, however, one does sleep better; and most people have reason to recognize a close relationship between satisfactory relaxation and ability to sleep."[1]

Feedback from workshop participants supports Rathbone's statement. Many participants report that specific relaxation techniques, or variations of techniques, have helped them to fall asleep. In addition, a commonly reported benefit of relaxation is that participants often sleep "more relaxed," feel more rested upon waking, and often find that they need fewer hours of sleep to feel refreshed. This new-found ability to sleep more easily and to feel more rested motivates many participants to continue daily relaxation.

Sleep and relaxation, it should be emphasized, although closely associated, are different states, and both are needed in adequate amounts. Sleep does not replace deep total body relaxation, and total body relaxation does not take the place of sleep. You must not think of one as a substitute for the other.

### Overcoming Insomnia

A common complaint of people who are tense is that they are unable to sleep readily and soundly. Many turn to therapy, medication, or drugs as aids to achieving sleep. Some find relief with these treatments, but many do not. Some ideas and techniques useful in improving sleep include ideas you can use to get in the right frame of mind for sleep and techniques that can be helpful in inducing sleep.

**Preparing for Sleep**   Your daily routine and bedtime habits may be contributing to your insomnia. If you are having trouble sleeping, you should take a look at your usual evening activities. Perhaps a change in habits or in attitudes will solve the problem.

**Reduce Physical and Mental Activity Before Bedtime**   A half hour to an hour before bedtime, begin to slow down. Perform tasks that are restful or even monotonous. Washing dishes, knitting, and light reading can help prepare you for sleep. If you find that television is stimulating or that the news often disturbs you, don't watch television late in the evening. Soothing background music can also be helpful and can accompany quiet tasks.

**Do Not Discuss Disturbing Topics Late in the Evening**   Financial problems, car or household repairs, difficulties at work, and other topics that may be disturbing should not be discussed late in the evening. These are likely to create irritation, frustration, anger, or tension. Set aside time earlier in the day for such discussions. This may sound easy, but many couples who have children and jobs find that the late evening hours are usually the only time they have alone together. And yet such people may find it especially helpful to avoid serious discussions late in the evening. Try to set aside some other time—perhaps a weekday lunch hour—for these talks.

**Plan the Next Day**   Many people, even those who normally sleep well, find it hard to sleep the night before a busy day. If this is a problem for you, you may find it helpful, before bedtime, to write out a schedule for the next day. Plan the day, listing everything you have to do and when you will do it. You will be less tense about the upcoming day once it is planned on paper. Being aware of everything that must be done and planning your activities will relieve your mind. You won't be worried about forgetting things and will sleep more peacefully.

This same procedure should be followed if you are already in bed and worry about the next day's activities or a creative idea pops into your mind. Get up, write down everything you are thinking about, and then go back to bed. You may want to keep a pad and pencil on a table next to your bed. Then you won't have to get out of bed to make notes about anything you don't want to forget.

**Don't Go to Bed until You are Tired**   We have become a society controlled by the clock. We eat, work, and sleep according to the clock. Too often people develop unsatisfactory sleep habits, because the body isn't tired when the clock says it is time to go to bed.

Say, for example, that rather than getting up at 6:30 A.M., as you usually do, that you sleep until 9:00 A.M., or you take a two-hour nap in the afternoon. When your normal bedtime comes, you go to bed because the clock says it's bedtime. However, your body may not be ready and you may have trouble sleeping. If this happens regularly, insomnia can become chronic, so that you have trouble sleeping even when you are tired.

One way to deal with this is to stay up until you are tired. Let your body determine when it needs sleep—not the clock. If you aren't tired until 1 or 2 A.M., don't go to sleep until then. But be sure to get up at your regular time and do not take a nap during the day. Stay out of the bedroom and off the sofa. Instead, try a fifteen or twenty minute relaxation break. After several days, you will find yourself getting back on a regular schedule and able to fall asleep more quickly when you go to bed.

**Never Go to Bed Angry**  The ability to express anger, negative feelings, and disappointment directly to the intended person is necessary for health and for healthy relationships. Communication skills are important if you want to express anger effectively and in nondestructive ways.

If anger has not been released effectively during the day, it is almost sure to build up and interfere with your ability to fall asleep quickly. Inhibition of anger can cause other difficulties, as well. Morris Holland and Gerald Tarlow have written:

> The extreme form of inhibiting anger is repression. The anger becomes unconscious and the person is not even aware that he or she is angry.
>
> What happens when anger becomes inhibited? Anxiety, depression, guilt, sleep problems, overwork, and other symptoms may be related to this stored-up reservoir of anger. Additionally, many psychologists believe that psychosomatic disorders, such as headaches, high blood pressure, and asthma may arise from inhibited angry emotions.[2]

It is natural to relive an argument or to plan in advance for the next confrontation with the individual with whom you are angry. These thoughts are likely to occur at night, when you lie in bed and reflect on the day's activities. And such thoughts are likely to interfere with sleep. When sleep does come, it is likely to be less sound and restful than it could be. Never go to bed angry—especially if the anger occurs late in the evening, just before you are about to retire.

**Increase Your Exercise Level During the Day**  Increasing one's daily exercise level, paradoxically, fosters relaxation and sleep. Exercise reduces muscular tension, and this makes it easier for the body to fall asleep. In addition, exercise tires the body, and this helps you sleep better.

**Soak in a Hot Tub**  Many people find that soaking in a hot tub is quite relaxing. To be effective, the water temperature must be comfortable. Soaking in hot water for relaxation and for various therapeutic reasons has been used for centuries. We have all read of the Roman baths and of various hot springs.

**Have a Massage**  A brief massage before bedtime often encourages sleep. Massage, which is a systematic manipulation of the soft tissues of the body, is thought by some to bring relief from physiological, psychological, and mechanical problems. Massage can be used for relaxation, for relief from pain, to facilitate recovery from after-effects of strenuous activity, and to encourage confidence. If a massage does any of these things for you, it can promote sleep.

## A Program for Sleep

Edmund Jacobson, in his book *You Must Relax*, lists factors that may be useful in eliminating sleepless nights. His "Program for Sleep" includes the following:

> If you have been sleepless and desire to learn to shut off your energies at night through relaxation:
> * Cultivate habits of relaxation at night and during daily activities.
> * Remember that a tense day is likely to be followed by a tense night.
> * Practice lying down for an hour near noon and near sundown.
> * Discontinue sedative medicines gradually as soon as your doctor permits.
> * Assume a fairly comfortable position, and if discomfort sets in do not shift repeatedly but relax in spite of discomfort.
> * Remember to keep up your daily drill [or relaxation exercises], or you may lose what gains you have made.
> * Do not be discouraged by relapses.
> * Above all, try to develop a complete let-go of the muscles of eyes and speech.
> * Learn to relax to some extent even in the presence of noises or other disturbances, including moderate distress and pain.[3]

Jacobson reminds us that insomnia that has occurred for only a brief period is easier to eliminate than is chronic insomnia:

> Individuals with severe chronic conditions, always associated with other symptoms of high nerve tension, are often unreasonable in their hopes of affecting a cure very promptly. They fail to understand that what they most require is a prolonged course in nervous reeducation. . . . While individuals vary greatly in the speed with which they learn to relax, a disordered condition such as insomnia that has lasted for many years commonly does not yield to treatment in less than one year and frequently requires a considerably longer time.[4]

## SLEEP-INDUCING TECHNIQUES

An often neglected side benefit of regular total body relaxation is an improved ability to fall asleep quickly and to sleep soundly. Many of the people who participate in relaxation programs report that they use these exercises as a means of relaxing—and then drift to sleep from this relaxed state.

Some of the exercises already described, or variations of them, can be used to improve sleep. There are two main reasons why relaxation techniques are useful for inducing sleep. First, a relaxed body is prepared for sleep; and second, when you focus your attention inward on a specific routine, you are less likely to think about outside stimuli or thoughts that would hinder the sleeping process.

## Exercise 36: Body Search for Sensations

This exercise is similar to the body search sensory awareness technique discussed previously.

### Exercise Description

- Assume your desired sleeping position. As you focus on your exhalation, exhale and relax.
- For two or three exhalations, focus on the supporting environment and allow the environment to support your body as you continue to exhale, and r-e-l-a-x.
- Following these exhalations, allow your attention to wander through the body. There is no set sequence, nor should you be in a hurry. As you "move" through the body, identify *any* sensations that you may feel or sense (heaviness, warmth, heartbeat, coolness, twitching, pressure, gurgling in the stomach or intestines, tension, stillness).
- Upon identifying a sensation, mentally acknowledge the sensation in your mind's eye and continue to wander through the body and passively search for others. You will notice that the number of sensations diminishes after a few minutes. As the mind continues to focus inward on the body, the mind will become quiet and sleep will result.
- Record your use of this exercise on the Practice Schedule Chart.

Practice Schedule Chart
Exercise 36: Body Search for Sensations

Goal:  To perform the body search for sensations exercise during each of
three practice sessions.

| Session | Date Performed | Exercise Time | Evaluation |
|---------|----------------|---------------|------------|
| 1       |                |               |            |
| 2       |                |               |            |
| 3       |                |               |            |

Total time spent on this exercise: _____

## Exercise 37: Body Search and the Breathing Rhythm

Exercise Description

- Assume your desired sleeping position. As you focus on your exhalations, exhale and relax.
- For two or three exhalations, focus on the supporting environment and allow the environment to support your body as you continue to exhale and r-e-l-a-x.
- Beginning at the head and moving downward, perform a body search for tension or movement. While focused on each body segment or muscle group, exhale and relax away any tensions you note.
- Upon completing the body search, focus on the exhalations only and as you exhale, relax, let go, and think or silently repeat the word "sleep" in time with each exhalation.
- As the mind begins to drift, allow nature to run its course. If sleep does not occur, you may want to combine this with one of the next three exercises.
- Record your use of this exercise on the Practice Schedule Chart.

Practice Schedule Chart
Exercise 37: Body Search and the Breathing Rhythm

Goal:   To perform the body search and breathing rhythm exercise during each of three practice sessions.

| Session | Date Performed | Exercise Time | Evaluation |
|---------|----------------|---------------|------------|
| 1       |                |               |            |
| 2       |                |               |            |
| 3       |                |               |            |

Total time spent on this exercise: _____

## Exercise 38: Breathing Rhythms

Exercise Description

- Assume your desired sleeping position. As you focus on your exhalations, exhale and relax.
- For two or three exhalations, focus on the supporting environment and allow the environment to support your body as you continue to exhale, and r-e-l-a-x.
- As you become more and more relaxed, focus on the exhalations and note the sensations (sinking down, slowing down, patience, heaviness, and others noted in Chapter 6) on each successive exhalation.
- Once relaxed, visualize the body's breath as being composed of colored vapors, and see the air flow into and out of the body. Do not force any sensation or visualization—allow them to happen. Focus only on the breath, and allow the body to breathe itself. Sleep will result naturally.
- Record your use of this exercise on the Practice Schedule Chart.

Practice Schedule Chart
Exercise 38: Breathing Rhythms

Goal:   To perform the breathing rhythms during each of three practice
sessions.

| Session | Date Performed | Exercise Time | Evaluation |
|---------|----------------|---------------|------------|
| 1 | | | |
| 2 | | | |
| 3 | | | |

Total time spent on this exercise: _____

## Exercise 39: Progressive Relaxation

Exercise Description

- Assume your desired sleeping position. As you focus on your exhalations, exhale and relax.
- For two or three exhalations, focus on the supporting environment and allow the environment to support your body as you continue to exhale, and r-e-l-a-x.
- Perform the progressive relaxation sequence discussed in Chapter 10. Begin with the smallest body part or muscle in one foot and continue to move your attention upward. As you reach the thigh of your starting leg, return to the toes of the opposite leg and repeat the same sequence. Relax each body part or muscle in time with your exhalations. Do not concern yourself with missed body parts or muscle groups.
- Keep your focus inward, and do not feel you must complete the exercise.
- Allow yourself to drift into sleep when the body and mind are ready.
- Record your use of this exercise on the Practice Schedule Chart.

Practice Schedule Chart
Exercise 39: Progressive Relaxation

Goal:   To perform the progressive relaxation exercise during each of three
practice sessions.

| Session | Date Performed | Exercise Time | Evaluation |
|---------|----------------|---------------|------------|
| 1       |                |               |            |
| 2       |                |               |            |
| 3       |                |               |            |

Total time spent on this exercise: _____

## Exercise 40: Counting Coupled with the Breathing Rhythm

Exercise Description

- Assume your desired sleeping position. As you focus on your exhalations, exhale and relax.
- For two or three exhalations, focus on the supporting environment and allow that environment to support your body as you continue to exhale, and r-e-l-a-x.
- As you continue to focus on the exhalation phase, count in sequence from one to ten and then from ten to one. Count one number per exhalation and repeat this sequence until sleep results.
- Variation: Count backward from ninety-nine until sleep results.
- Record your use of this exercise on the Practice Schedule Chart.

Practice Schedule Chart

Exercise 40: Counting Coupled with the Breathing Rhythm

Goal:   To perform the counting coupled with the breathing rhythm exercise during each of three practice sessions.

| Session | Date Performed | Exercise Time | Evaluation |
|---------|---------------|---------------|------------|
| 1 | | | |
| 2 | | | |
| 3 | | | |

Total time spent on this exercise: _____

## SUMMARY

Practical relaxation skills are designed to be used in situations in which you would not ordinarily relax. They may not provide the physiological benefits of total body relaxation, but they can help you to manage and control stress, and they conserve energy that would be consumed if you were under stress.

The term *differential relaxation* is most often used when describing a group of practical relaxation skills. Differential relaxation involves learning to differentiate between muscle tensions that are required to perform a particular task and muscular tensions that are not needed to perform that task. These exercises can be performed in almost any position—even while you are walking, running, or engaged in a sport.

Insomnia and restlessness can also be combated through the use of relaxation. Success varies depending on the type, longevity, and duration of the problem. And there are a number of things you can do to prepare yourself for a restful night. These include (1) reducing the level of your activity—both physical and mental—prior to bedtime, (2) avoiding discussions of disturbing topics late in the evening, (3) planning the upcoming day, (4) not going to bed until you are tired, (5) not going to bed angry, (6) increasing exercise level during the day, (7) soaking in a hot tub, and (8) having a massage.

## Notes

1 Josephine L. Rathbone, *Relaxation* (Philadelphia: Lea and Febiger, 1969), p. 132.
2 M. K. Holland and G. Tarlow, *Using Psychology: Principles of Behavior and Your Life* (Boston: Little, Brown, 1980), pp. 181–182.
3 Edmund Jacobson, *You Must Relax* (New York: McGraw-Hill, 1976), p. 111.
4 Ibid., p. 110.

## References

Brown, Barbara B. *Stress and the Art of Biofeedback.* New York: Harper & Row, 1977.

Jacobson, Edmund. *Your Must Relax.* New York: McGraw-Hill, 1976.

Rathbone, Josephine L. *Relaxation.* Philadelphia: Lea & Febiger, 1969.

Tappan, F. M. *Healing Message Techniques: A Study of Eastern and Western Methods.* Reston Publishing Company, 1978.

# 13

████████████

# COMMUNICATION

## MISUNDERSTANDING AND STRESS

The word communicate means "to make common." More technically, communication is defined as "a person sending a message to another individual with the conscious intent of evoking a response."[1] The primary concern of communication is to take an idea, find symbols (usually in the form of words, voice tones, postures, and gestures) that will express the idea, and make that idea common with another person.

In other words, an effective communicator takes a thought or feeling and turns it into a message made up of symbols. These symbols transmit the message to another person in a way that enables the other person to interpret the message as intended. When a problem occurs anywhere in this process and results in a misunderstanding or misinterpretation of the message, there is a breakdown in communication. This breakdown is likely to create stress.

In Chapter 4, we discussed stress as a reaction—a reaction to a stressor. The inability to transmit or receive the intended message accurately can cause a reaction, and this breakdown in communication becomes a stressor. Communication as a stressor then can elicit the stress response.

Many factors can cause the stress reaction during a breakdown in the communication process, and it is not possible to cover all of these factors here. However, one element is common to all of these factors. This is the element of *perception*. Words do not cause stress, nor do voice, tone, pitch, or nonverbal gestures or symbols. It is the perception, the interpretation, the possible threat of these components of the communication process, that can elicit the stress response. How we perceive these symbols triggers our emotions, and our emotions then trigger the physical arousal. And, as is true of all emotionally-induced stress, this stress is based on past experiences. So it is not failure of the process, not fear, anger, or frustration that are important. These are underlying factors, secondary to the primary cause. The primary cause is the perception of the event. That perception sets off the anger and frustration.

The emotional arousal may be due to one or a combination of the following:

1. Failure to say what we intend
   a. not selecting appropriate phrases that make our thoughts common with another person
   b. not having the opportunity to voice our thoughts and feelings
   c. not being willing to say what we want to say
2. Fear
   a. fear of rejection if we say the wrong thing—or say something in the wrong way
   b. fear of reprisal
3. Expectation—anticipating or expecting a certain response (remember, evoking a response does *not* mean evoking an anticipated response—it refers to allowing the other person to respond)
4. Anger—which is often a secondary reaction (the primary reaction is usually a hurt feeling or a bruised self-concept, and anger is the emotional reaction to the primary reaction)
5. Frustration—usually a secondary reaction (the primary reaction may be the inability to express oneself clearly, or not having the opportunity to do so)

Each of these factors can initiate the emotional response that then evokes the stress response within the body.


## EFFECTIVE COMMUNICATION

Effective communication means taking a thought or feeling, turning it into a message, and transmitting the message to another person so that the person interprets the message as intended (Figure 13-1). The message is transmitted to the receiver by word symbols, body postures, voice tones, voice fluctuations, and gestures. The message travels visually or through the sound

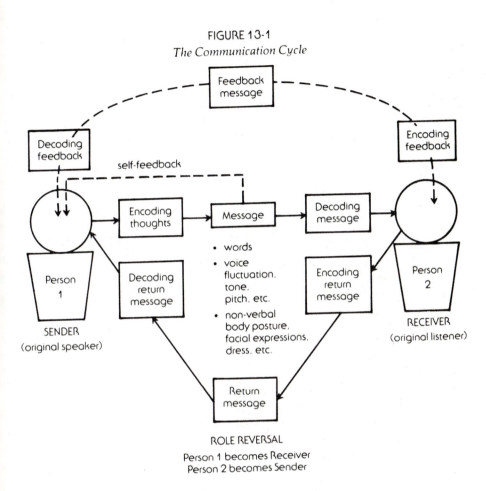

FIGURE 13-1

*The Communication Cycle*

waves. Many of the body senses are involved in sending and receiving messages, and it is important to be aware of all of these when trying to communicate.

## The Message

The message is a factor in communication breakdown because what is conveyed is influenced by how the message is transmitted. A message is conveyed in three different ways: (1) with word symbols, (2) with voice tone and fluctuation, and (3) by nonverbal means (usually referred to as body language, or as nonverbal communication).

**Word Symbols**   Most people assume that word symbols are the major component in the transmission of a message, but research results suggest that this is not true. Word symbols actually account for the smallest percentage of a transmitted message. Words convey roughly 7 percent of the message. The major problems with word symbols are the words chosen, the grammatical form used, and lack of verbal ability. Of the three ways in which the message is transmitted (word symbols, voice tone and inflection, and nonverbal means), word symbols are probably the strongest modality for most people. However, breakdowns can and do occur because of poor word selection. When these breakdowns occur, the stress response can be initiated if some form of emotional arousal is produced.

**Voice**   The voice tone, pitch, and fluctuation account for about 38 percent of the transmitted message. The cliche, "It's not what is said but how it is said" is certainly accurate. When communicating, you should be aware of your voice and how you use it. Remember, your voice conveys a good portion of the message. Nonawareness can result in breakdowns that will diminish your effectiveness and contribute to increased stress.

**Nonverbal Means**   The last component of the message is the nonverbal portion of the message. This component is probably the least understood of the three, yet it accounts for the major portion of the transmitted message—about 55 percent. Nonverbal symbols are often referred to as body language. Julius Fast, author of *Body Language,* discusses "any nonreflexive or reflexive movement of a part, or all of the body, used by a person to communicate an emotional message to the outside world."[2] Body language includes both body posture and facial expression.

    In communicating effectively with others, a mastery of nonverbal communication may be more important than verbal fluency. Nonverbal communications include dress, physique, posture, body tension, facial expression, eye contact, hand and body movements, distance, touch, and mannerisms. To communicate effectively, you must be aware of the importance of nonverbal clues and able to use nonverbal symbols effectively. If you are oblivious to these, you are likely to send conflicting messages that result in communication breakdown. Perhaps Bernard Gunther described nonverbal communication most effectively when he stated:

    Nonverbal communication is:

    Shaking hands
    Your posture
    Facial expressions

Your appearance
Voice tone
Hair style
Your clothes
Your gestures
The expression in your eyes
Your smile
How close you stand to others
How you listen
Your confidence
Your breathing
Your breath
Your manners
Your mannerisms
The way you move
The way you stand
How you touch other people

These aspects of you affect your relationship with other people, often without you and them realizing it.[3]

## Ways to Facilitate Understanding

It is important, when we communicate with one another, that we make an effort to understand—that we care enough about each other to make the effort to communicate clearly. This means being receptive, and it means using your knowledge of the other person when choosing the words, voice, and gestures with which you communicate. It is important, also, to listen with care as well as with understanding and interest.

**Mutual Awareness**   Walk a mile in my shoes! It's easier said than done. No one can walk in my shoes. I bring with me unique experiences—no one else has the same collection of experiences that I have. The same is true of you. For me to assume that my experiences are the same as yours can only hinder the communication process. Kenneth Olson has illustrated this point, in *Can You Wait Until Friday?*, with the paragraph below. As you read the paragraph, try to figure out who is being described.

> On a cold January day, a forty-three-year-old man was sworn in as chief executive of his country. By his side stood his predecessor, a famous general, who fifteen years previously had commanded his country's armed forces in a war which resulted in a total defeat of the German nation. The young man was brought up in the Roman Cath-

olic faith. After the ceremony, there was a five-hour parade in his honor, and he stayed up until 3:00 A.M. celebrating.[4]

Most Americans reading the above paragraph and analyzing the facts presented are likely to think of the inauguration of John F. Kennedy as the thirty-fifth president of the United States. This assumption is based on our backgrounds and experiences. However, the above paragraph is an account of the installation of Adolf Hitler as chancellor of Germany in 1933. This is an example of how one can misinterpret even facts if one assumes that "I know what you mean" and "You know what I said." In interpersonal relationships, assumptions can impede the communication process to the point of breakdown.

As you communicate, try to recognize that the person you are communicating with is unique. There is not another person in the world with the same genetic makeup and the same experiences. Recognize that the other person does not perceive the world exactly as you do. This will help prevent possible breakdowns. It is important, for effective communications, never to make assumptions.

**Empathy**   Empathy is the ability to experience or participate in the feelings or ideas of another person. To empathize, you need to try to understand the other person—to listen inside me as I listen to you. It requires that I not only hear what is said, but also how it is said—and what is not said—to be sure that "what I heard is what you said."

## Listening

One of the most effective ways to improve communication is to listen carefully. Listening is generally used more than the other major components of communication during a typical day. Yet, oddly enough, listening is one of the least developed of the communicative skills.

Just because a person can hear does not necessarily mean that he can listen, or that he will listen. Yet we each have two ears and only one mouth. Kenneth Olson states, "Show me a good listener, and I'll show you a kind and warm person; a good mother, a good father, and a good lover. Show me a good listener, and I'll show you a winner—someone who has the ability to make people feel that they are for real."[5] Do you know someone who is a good listener? Does that person stand out from other people because of this quality? Is that person enjoyable to be around? Does he or she make you feel that you are for real? Listening is a skill that needs to be nourished by each of us. It is important to hear what others wish to make common with us.

Listening is a skill that can be improved if you only take the time to understand the act of listening and make a conscious effort to become a better listener. The listener brings to the listening situation a variety of experiences. We use past experiences and the rules that we have learned to apply in communication situations when we interpret any message. Keep in mind that listening behavior is governed by the same principles that govern all of our behaviors.

Effective listening involves putting aside expectations, first impressions, and premature judgments about both the speaker and the topic. True listening means listening with an open mind. The individual who truly listens risks being changed or discovering that the other person's way of doing things or of thinking may be more effective and more valid than his or her own. Effective listening involves personal risk. We may open ourselves to change that we do not want because it conflicts with ideas, patterns, or prejudices. Many people, consciously or unconsciously, are not ready to take such risks.

**Active Listening**  Active listening is listening with a purpose—it means involvement. The active listener tunes into not only the message but also the feelings of the sender. The listener who empathizes is likely to have a clear understanding of the message. As we tune into the entire message more fully, we can put our understanding of the message into our own words and feed it back to the sender for verification (feedback).

Thus, active listening can help to diminish the number and extent of breakdowns, and of potential stressors, in the communication cycle. It allows us to tune into the message closely, assess the entire message (word symbols, voice, and nonverbal symbols), become more aware of the feelings of the sender, and continually verify and clarify our interpretation and understanding of the message through feedback. Active listening can eliminate many of the major barriers to effective communication.

**Listening Skills**  Since listening skills are essential for effective communication, we will examine seven basic principles that can be useful in improving listening skills. Improved listening skills help increase effectiveness of interpersonal communication and reduce potential stressors.

*Principle One: You must want to listen.* Enter the conversation with interest. Listening can be challenging, fun, and enlightening, if we want to listen and make the effort to listen carefully.

*Principle Two: Stop talking.* Obviously, you can't listen effectively if you are talking at the same time. Show respect for the speaker—listen without interrupting. Don't carry on parallel monologues. True dialogue requires listening.

*Principle Three: Don't argue mentally or prepare your response.* Listen! After the other person has completed what he or she wants to say, you will have time to respond. Many great speakers, debators, and politicians pause before responding to a question. This allows them to respond to the entire message, rather than to just a part of it. If you don't hear the whole message and respond to only part of it, your answer reveals that. Unfortunately, many people find silence, no matter how short it is, uncomfortable. If you prepare your response while the other person is still talking, so that silence will be eliminated, you may miss an important part of the message— and as a result your response may be inappropriate.

*Principle Four: Act like a good listener!* Sit attentively, be alert but relaxed, ask questions, nod your head, and encourage the speaker to continue. Does this sound hard? Use the feedback cycle to clarify and check out your interpretations and ask "furthering" questions, such as "How did that happen?" or "Was any one hurt?" or "Were you there while it was happening?" At the same time, you can nod your head, raise your eyebrows, and make both verbal and nonverbal responses to what is being said. If you look and act as if you enjoy listening, eventually you will not only improve your enjoyment but you will become a more effective listener.

*Principle Five: Get rid of distractions.* Put away papers, pens, pencils, paper clips, watches, and other things that prevent you from giving the speaker your undivided attention. When you do this, you will find that the speakers often respond more clearly. It is distracting for the speaker to see you doodling, tapping a pencil on the table to the tune "Is that all there is," and glancing at your watch every few seconds. Many people feel annoyed and, in a sense, ignored by this kind of behavior.

*Principle Six: Concentrate on what the speaker is telling you.* Empathize with the speaker; put yourself in the speaker's place. Listen not only to what is said, but also to how it is said and to what is not said. The speaker is a unique person. Try to understand the speaker and the speaker's feelings.

*Principle Seven: Check your perception of what you hear.* As you listen, ask yourself, "Do I really understand what is being said?" "Should I check it out to be sure my interpretation is accurate?" Remember—if in doubt, check it out!

## OBSTACLES TO EFFECTIVE COMMUNICATION

Several common pitfalls hinder effective communications. Listed and discussed here are some of the most troublesome obstacles.

## Labeling

Try not to label either the speaker or the topic. The individual who classifies or labels a person or a topic cannot be an unbiased participant in interpersonal communications. Labeling and stereotyping may seem to simplify your understanding of a subject, but in reality they obscure your perception of what the speaker is saying.

## Jumping to Conclusions

Listen to the speaker until he or she finishes. Do not jump to conclusions or interrupt the speaker or assume that you know what is going to be said. Most assumptions are not totally correct. Even if they are correct, it is rude to interrupt. The speaker may well be offended by an interruption, and the negative feelings generated will interfere with clear communication.

## Becoming Defensive

Defensiveness usually results from feelings of inferiority, insecurity, or hurt. The individual who feels he or she has been attacked verbally and whose ego is bruised is likely to become defensive. Once emotions become involved, an immediate reaction is to strike back, to establish a position. The counterattack seems justified by the hurt that provoked it. If you become irritated while listening, sit back and continue to listen—and then process your interpretations and check them for accuracy. Too often, we become defensive and strike back, even though the speaker is offering a legitimate viewpoint or a constructive criticism. The old notion of counting to ten before you react in anger can reduce stress by giving you time to think about what is being said. When you have the urge to react defensively, try to keep quiet and continue to listen. Once you hear the speaker out, you will have a better basis for responding. Often you will find that tuning into the breathing cycle and exhalations for a few breaths is all that is necessary (see Chapter 12).

## An Unsuitable Environment

There is a time and a place for everything. Casual conversation can take place almost anywhere. But an important conversation requires a suitable environment. Some environments are not conducive to effective communication. An appropriate environment is one that is acceptable to the parties involved. Some people can communicate effectively in a noisy restaurant, while others find that they cannot communicate in any environment if they are sitting around a table.

## SUMMARY

To communicate is to make common. An effective communicator takes an idea or feeling, finds symbols that express it accurately, and then conveys the idea or feeling to another person. The inability to transmit or receive the intended message accurately can produce stress. Stress is elicited not only by the symbols or lack of symbols used by the speaker but also by the listener's perception and interpretation of the message. If the listener feels threatened or hurt, that reaction triggers emotions that in turn trigger the physical arousal.

Effective communication involves transmitting a message through word symbols, voice symbols, and nonverbal means. To transmit a message effectively, you need to be aware of the other person, you need to bring empathy to the communication process, and you need to be an active listener.

An effective, active listener (1) wants to listen, (2) stops talking, (3) doesn't argue mentally or prepare a response while the other person is talking, (4) acts like a good listener, (5) eliminates distractions, (6) concentrates on what the speaker is saying, and (7) checks out his or her interpretation of what is said.

Obstacles to effective communication include labeling, jumping to conclusions, becoming defensive, and trying to communicate in an unsuitable environment. Effective communication does not just happen. It is a skill that can be developed by anyone who wants to communicate effectively. The individual who is able to communicate clearly and listen carefully is likely to reduce stress and reduce the likelihood that he or she will contribute to the stress of others.

## Notes

1 David W. Johnson, *Reaching Out: Interpersonal Effectiveness and Self-Actualization* (Englewood Cliffs, N. J.: Prentice-Hall, 1972), p. 61.

2 Julius Fast, *Body Language* (New York: Pocket Books, 1971), p. 2.

3 Bernard Gunther, *Sense Relaxation* (New York: Collier Books, 1968), p. 90.

4 Kenneth Olson, *Can You Wait Until Friday?* (Greenwich: Fawcett Publications, 1975), p. 52.

5 Ibid., p. 46.

## References

Berne, Eric. *Transactional Analysis in Psychotherapy.* New York: Grove Press, 1961.

Berne, Eric. *What Do You Say After You Say Hello?* New York: Grove Press, 1972.

Fast, Julius. *Body Language.* New York: Pocket Books, 1971.

Gordon, T. *Parent Effectiveness Training.* New York: Peter H. Wyden, 1970.

Gunther, Bernard. *Sense Relaxation.* New York: Collier Books, 1968.

Harris, Thomas A. *I'm O.K. — You're O.K.* New York: Harper & Row, 1969.

Johnson, David W. *Reaching Out: Interpersonal Effectiveness and Self-Actualization.* Englewood Cliffs, N. J.: Prentice-Hall, 1972.

Olson, Kenneth. *Can You Wait Until Friday?* Greenwich: Fawcett Publications, 1975.

# 14

# TIME
# MANAGEMENT

In one way or another, everything discussed in this book involves time. Your time. Time to read, to practice relaxation exercises, to reflect, to be alive. Time is what is used to experience life. Unfortunately, time can be a curse, a devastating stressor. In Chapter 2, it was established that simply being alive involves having some stress. Could it be, however, that in pursuit of a more effective twenty-four-hour day, the amount of time devoted to the various aspects of life and the quality of that time can make a difference in how much stress you encounter? Does it make any difference how you use the time spent in personal, vocational, and family pursuits? How does ineffective use of time lead to stress? Are there ways to improve your use of time? In this chapter relationships between time and stress are described, and an approach to time management and ways to overcome some of the major obstacles to using time effectively are presented.

## TIME AND STRESS

There are three major areas where time is a factor and potential stressor—in the time you devote to yourself, to your family, and to your vocation. Potential stressors in one area can also affect another area. To illustrate this relationship, look at Paul's life in the context of the Personal Satisfaction Index[1] (Table 14-1). This index lists potential stressors to self, family, and vocation. Continuums for each potential stressor and area have been developed. At the far left (-) of the continuum the potential stressor is a problem, while at the far right (+) it is not. The continuums are presented without numbers because it is important for you to notice only tendencies in and relationships among the three areas. Remember: It is your perception of events that determines your reaction to them.

When Paul completed the Personal Satisfaction Index, under job he marked priorities, procrastination, and achievement to the left of center. One scenario for Paul's responses reads like this: Paul takes the time to look ahead, to plan for the future. He has identified job-related tasks that need to be accomplished in the next month. However, Paul has not taken the time to rank order these tasks, to determine which need to be completed first or which will bring him the most personal satisfaction. As a result, Paul spends much of his time performing insignificant tasks while ignoring a major task his supervisors are counting on. Perhaps Paul is intimidated by the important task, afraid he will not be able to do it properly, and so is procrastinating. As the completion time nears Paul realizes that the job must be done and so, under pressure, he jumps into the task. All of his energies are now directed toward the completion of the large task. But because he is short of time, Paul does less than a desirable job, or worse yet, a job that Paul perceives as less than a good effort. He knows that he could have done a better job if he "only had more time to complete the project."

Other areas of Paul's life are also affected. When Paul realizes that he is running out of time, he begins to spend evenings and Saturdays—time that is usually spent with family, friends, or in personal pursuits—at the office. His wife and children feel neglected because Paul is home so little and is tired when he is home. And Paul, because he is preoccupied and tired when he is home, is irritated and frustrated by their demands. And he has no time at all for his own needs. Thus, Paul's use—or misuse—of time produces stressful conditions in all areas of his life.

If you were to complete Table 14-1, what observations would you make about your perceived satisfaction on each continuum? Do these observations suggest where potential sources of stress may be and how those relate to your use of time?

## KINDS OF STRESS CAUSED BY POOR TIME MANAGEMENT

If the way you are using time is different from the way you would like to be using time, the discrepancy is likely to cause conflict—especially if you are not making progress toward goals you have set for yourself. Such conflict is

TABLE 14-1
*Personal Satisfaction Index*

Listed here are potential stressors related to self, family, job. After you understand the explanation of each stressor, place an X on the continuum for self, family, job, where appropriate: toward the ( − ) if the stressor is a serious one for you, toward the ( + ) if the stressor is not a serious one for you. Be as honest in your assessment as possible as no one will view these assessments but yourself. If a potential stressor does not apply to a continuum column for you, simply leave the column blank.

*Explanation of Stressor*

GOALS: The process of formally establishing broad based statements about what you want to accomplish. It is the direction given to long-term, short-term, or intermediate aspirations.

PLANNING: The act of establishing effective control over your own future.

PRIORITIES: Conscious and systematic thought and ranking given to the importance of specific tasks to be accomplished.

PACING: The ability to maintain a steady rate of progress toward goals without extremes of high or low activity.

PROCRASTINATION: The putting off of something that needs to be done and isn't getting the attention needed.

DELEGATION: The process of entrusting responsibility and authority to another who will act as your representative.

EXPECTATIONS: Anticipating the future from a realistic perspective.

COMMUNICATION: The act of "making common" with another person's thoughts, feelings, or desires.

RELAXATION: The systematic means used to quiet mental and physical processes.

LEISURE TIME: The free, unoccupied time when the only demands are self-imposed.

SPIRITUALITY: Defining, refining, and integrating value and moral systems into life experiences.

ACHIEVEMENT: Making satisfactory progress toward goals according to assets and limitations.

RELATIONSHIPS: The relative satisfaction derived from positive interactions with others.

VOCATION: The relative satisfaction derived from current work pursuits.

LOCATION: The relative satisfaction derived from living in a particular geographical and/or cultural environment.

COMMITMENTS: Staying with and following through on perceived priorities.

ASSERTIVENESS: The ability to deal with people and events in a positive and direct manner without feeling guilty.

WORRY: The act of using the imagination in a nonproductive manner to think or visualize about something in the future.

Table 14-1 continued

| Potential Stressors | − | Self | + | − | Family | + | − | Job | + |
|---|---|---|---|---|---|---|---|---|---|
| Goals | | | | | | | | | |
| Planning | | | | | | | | | |
| Priorities | | | | | | | | | |
| Pacing | | | | | | | | | |
| Procrastination | | | | | | | | | |
| Delegation | | | | | | | | | |
| Expectations I have for myself | | | | | | | | | |
| Expectations others have for me | | | | | | | | | |
| Communication | | | | | | | | | |
| Relaxation | | | | | | | | | |
| Leisure time | | | | | | | | | |
| Spirituality | | | | | | | | | |
| Achievement | | | | | | | | | |
| Relationships | | | | | | | | | |
| Vocation | | | | | | | | | |
| Location | | | | | | | | | |
| Commitments | | | | | | | | | |
| Assertiveness | | | | | | | | | |
| Worry | | | | | | | | | |

likely to result from: (1) hurry sickness and time pressures, which cause you to feel rushed and living out of "pace" with your own body rhythm; (2) anxiety and worry, which keep the stress response elicited as you fret about getting everything done; (3) dissatisfaction and frustration, which result when you are not moving toward established goals or have no goals to move toward; and (4) negative cycles, which keep you immobilized and unable to make the best use of time.

Conflict that results from any of these causes produces stress, and stress encountered in one aspect of life has a tendency to affect other aspects. The kinds of problems that result from these conflicts are determined by the individual's personality and life experience as well as by the current circumstances of the person's life. But all of us can profit from an examination of our values, goals, and priorities as we attempt to apportion our time productively.

You can use relaxation to intervene and slow the pace at which you live. When you find yourself saying that you don't have time to relax, that's when you need to relax the most. Toffler has used the word "velocity," Pelletier used "jet lag," and Friedman used "hurry sickness" to describe the pace of modern life. The real speeder (Friedman's Type A person[2]) often fails to perceive that a person's time can be exhausted by his or her activities. As a consequence, the person never ceases trying to "stuff" more and more activities into each day. How are you affected by the three Cs—clocks, calendars, and completion times? If you find yourself controlled by these, you are likely to find yourself subjected to stress from one or more of the following:

1.  *Preoccupation with things to be accomplished.* This makes it difficult to concentrate on the task at hand and may lead to poor quality results. If you are thinking about all the things you need to get done, you are likely to jump from one activity to another without completing any one task and without thinking carefully about which is most important for personal or professional satisfaction.

2.  *Ineffective pacing.* If you work in spurts and expend high energy in an effort to meet deadlines, your body is thrown out of balance, and adjustment is needed. Rhythm is broken and, if intervention doesn't occur, stress is imminent. Over a long period of time, various health problems may result.

3.  *Stimulus overload.* If you have too much to do in the time available, you are likely to become dissatisfied. Dissatisfaction precipitates frustration. Dissatisfaction and frustration can lead to lethargy, which makes effective time use even more difficult. Or you may spend more

time and energy trying to get control of things only to discover that it is impossible, resulting in more intense feelings of frustration.

4. *Stimulus underload.* Having too much time might seem desirable, especially when you are suffering from stimulus overload. Yet not having enough to do may result in boredom, listlessness, anxiety, and dissatisfaction—any of which may elicit the stress response. Hans Selye writes that "among people engaged in the most common occupations of modern society—the lower and middle echelons of business, industry, agriculture, and public life, from the simple handyman to the administrator or public servant with limited responsibilities—one of the major sources of distress arises from dissatisfaction with life, namely, from disrespect for their own accomplishments."[3]

5. *Anxiety.* Anxiety is a vague, often unidentified feeling that something is wrong. It can range in intensity from uneasiness to panic. Anxiety keeps the stress response activated long after homeostasis should have been restored.

6. *Negative cycles.* A combination of any of the first five points can generate a negative stress cycle. Too much to do can feed hurry sickness or poor pacing. Hurry sickness or poor pacing may leave you feeling frustrated and unable to use time effectively. When you don't get the most out of available time, things pile up, and you continually have too much to do. Then you don't feel good about yourself, your accomplishments, or the direction your life is heading. Even efforts to break out of a negative cycle can cause stress (remember: this too is an adjustment) until body balance is restored and normal rhythm is reestablished.

These six stresses may result from inability to use time to achieve a desired level of satisfaction. Satisfaction is needed in each of the three areas—self, family, and job. If you allow yourself to be controlled by the clock, calendar, and completion times, you are likely to use personal time for your job. This can affect the quality of time spent with your family and friends. Frustration may set in and feed a negative cycle.

## AN APPROACH TO TIME MANAGEMENT

"Time is Life. To waste your time is to waste your life; to manage your time is to manage your life. Each person has twenty-four hours each day, 168 hours each week—no more and no less."[23] This means that time is a valuable, nonrenewable commodity. You cannot use less today and save some to use tomorrow. Today, right now, this very minute is the only time you can count on. The time in each person's life is for experiencing and making the most out of the here and now. John Hoyt has described time as a bank account:

> If you had a bank that credited your account each morning with $86,400—
>
> That carried over no balance from day to day—
>
> Allowed you to keep no cash in your account—
>
> And every evening cancelled whatever part of the amount you had failed to use during the day—
>
> What would you do?
>
> Draw out every cent every day, of course, and use it to your advantage!
>
> Well, you have such a bank—and its name is "TIME."
>
> Every morning, it credits you with 86,400 seconds. Every night, it rules off as lost whatever of this you have failed to invest to good purpose.
>
> It carries over no balances.
>
> It allows no overdrafts.
>
> Each day, it opens a new account with you.
>
> Each night, it burns the records of the day.
>
> If you fail to use the day's deposits, the loss is yours.
>
> There is no going back.
>
> There is no drawing against the "Tomorrow."
>
> It is up to each of us to invest this precious fund of hours, minutes and seconds in order to get from it the utmost in health, happiness, and success![4]

Time is what each person doesn't have enough of, yet each person has all that is necessary. It is life, and we know that we have a finite amount of that. If you want to manage time better to reduce its threat as a stressor, then you have to improve the way you manage the experiences and opportunities of your life.

In *Controlling Stress and Tension,* Daniel Girdano and George Everly describe time management as "the process by which you can set priorities and schedule tasks into the most efficient order possible."[5] To do this you need to be aware of your values and clear about your goals. And you need to be willing to take the time to think about each of the three areas of your life (self, family, and vocation) and to set priorities in each.

If you are to manage your time effectively, you must also learn to pace yourself. As you learn to manage your time, you will find that you can control, and even eliminate, stimulus overload, stimulus underload, ineffective use of time, anxiety, worry, and negative cycles.

## Values

Values are what we believe in; they are chosen freely, and they are lived consistently. Values, as well as dreams and hopes, are found in what John Pilch calls one's "inner space." Inner space is the very core of one's being, the fibers that hold the person together. It is that sacred place in each person where one tries to put purpose and meaning to life and direct that life through what are truly authentic human pleasures and joyous experiences.[6]

Socrates said that an unexamined life was a life not worth living. Examination is one way of trying to discover more about who we are, where we are heading in life, and how we are going to get there. But how many of us have taken the time to seriously examine the purpose, the meaning, the direction of our lives, and to make sense out of what oftentimes doesn't appear to have any sense to it? We spend so much time working to enjoy the good life that we don't have enough time to think about what we mean by the good life. Working hard consumes time. If we are to live the good life and reduce stress, some time must be used for self-examination.

John Pilch has stated that "wellness is directly related to your purpose in life."[7] As you continue to experience life, grow, and change, your purposes and directions change. Tables 14-2 and 14-3 contain questions that can help you to examine your life. Take time for introspection as you think about these questions.

## Goals

Managing the time of your life and reducing stress definitely includes reviewing your goals. Goals are statements about what you want to accomplish with your time. Goals can be long term, short term, or intermediate. They can be goals for self, vocation, or family. Goals provide direction and help you to keep track of your progress. It is useful to list goals, long term and short term, for yourself, your vocation, and your family. When listing goals, put down everything that comes to mind. You can rank goals after you have listed all of them. Remember: These are only broad statements. As you grow, change, or reach a goal, you may want to make revisions or add new goals. It is important to remain flexible, but you don't want to lose sight of your long-range destination.

TABLE 14-2
*Purpose in Life*

---

*What is your goal, your whole reason for living?*
*What do you want to do with your life?*

---

What does *society* suggest: getting married? getting divorced? having a family? not having children? going to college? making a lot of money?

What purpose does your *family* or *ethnic background* assign to life?

Who taught you about life's meaning, purposes, goals?

What have you decided about life's goals for yourself?

---

SOURCE: John J. Pilch, "Spiritual Wellness Reflection Guide" (Paper distributed at the University of Wisconsin–La Crosse, 1979).

TABLE 14-3
*Pleasures, Joys, Satisfactions*

*Which of life's pleasures do you cherish most?*

Are these appropriate pleasures? Why? Which would you add (or subtract)?

Do you ever deny yourself or give up pleasures for any reason at any time? When? Why?

How much fun do you get out of life? What gives you the greatest pleasure in living? the least?

How do *you* judge whether your happiness in life is truly satisfying and fulfilling?

SOURCE: John J. Pilch, "Spiritual Wellness Reflection Guide" (Paper distributed at the University of Wisconsin–La Crosse, 1979).

Edward Dayton describes two kinds of goals—"be" goals and "do" goals. "Be" and "do" goals should be made for each category of self, family, and work. The "be" goals are determined by your values and standards and include personal qualities you want to develop. These goals are expressed in your relationships with other people, and progress toward them is found in the feedback received from others.[8]

"Do" goals are what you want to accomplish. It is useful to plan specific steps toward each of these goals.

Every goal is connected to the other goals. Time is the connecting factor, because you must apportion how much time will be devoted to the steps that move you closer to the goals. From this perspective, then, managing time and one's life and reducing time pressures as a stressor involves establishing priorities and sticking to these priorities with some degree of consistency.

## Priorities

No one can tell you what your priorities are or should be. You must decide which tasks are most important and which can wait. You know what your long-term goals are and what your values are. If you do not take the time to think about your goals and values and to establish priorities—to rank your tasks and activities—you are likely to experience stress.

Without an organized and systematic way of ranking what is important for yourself, work, and family, it is easy to get caught spending your time (that means life) on someone else's priorities or wasting time. When this happens, you worry about how to cram more and more things to do in less and less time. Anxiety develops, frustration sets in, and you move a lot faster but still don't accomplish what you set out to do. It is possible at this point for a primary/secondary stress cycle to get started. How is your time organized and how are the tasks ranked to cover the experiences of each day, week, month in an effort to avoid needless stress? If you are not sure where you are going, there is a good chance that you will end up somewhere else.

There seems to be a lot of truth in the old statement that "the hardest part of any job is getting started." It doesn't seem to matter if the task is large or small, overwhelming or distasteful. Often it is just plain hard to get started, especially if you aren't sure which task is most important.

The ABC method, or a similar method of setting priorities, allows you to see what you view as important and what can be eliminated, or at least postponed. This method includes listing what you would like to do or what needs to be done each day, week, or month, for yourself, work, and family.

Next to each high priority item you place an A; a C is placed next to each low or unimportant item; and a B is placed next to the remaining items. If you have difficulty deciding whether an item is an A or B, make it a B. If you aren't sure if an item is a B or a C, make it a C. Sooner or later, it will become clear which it really is.

Don't worry about your ranking. Priorities, like goals, can be changed to meet the requirements of emergencies, conflicts, and compromise. Remember: your friends or spouse or boss may not agree with your rankings. You can reduce stress by remaining flexible and open for compromise if priorities need to be changed.

The ABC method of setting priorities helps you to see where you should be spending the most time. It also tells you which items—the Cs—have the potential to be time robbers. If you aren't sure whether a C item should be done, ask yourself, "What will happen to me if I don't do the C?" If your answer is "nothing" or "very little," then you can probably skip the C and use that time for As and Bs. If that C is important to someone else, that person will communicate that to you. Then you may decide to make that item a B or an A. This flexibility reduces time pressure and the stress it produces.

Let's look at a day in the life of one man, Fred. Fred teaches at a university. On this particular day, Fred lists these items and then ranks them:

C-2 Write catalog description change and send to department chairperson

A-1 Prepare for 402 class

A-1 Teach class

C-4 Respond to letter from Department of Public Instruction Standards

A-4 Jog

B-1 Meet with Jane about upcoming workshop

B-2 Write paper to present at conference

C-3 Respond to information request from Daryl

A-2 Relax

B-1 Prepare slides and handout for workshop

C-1 Write follow-up letters to teachers

Preparation for and teaching of his class were ranked A and the most important of the As. Fred is concerned about keeping his job, about salary adjustments, and about personal satisfaction. But look at the A-2s. On the surface, these might seem questionable, but to Fred they are important. Fred jogs to control weight, to manage stress, and to feel better. He jogs in the middle of the day because it puts him in a good frame of mind for the afternoon. Fred also maintains that the stamina and endurance developed from jogging have added about two hours to his day, time he spends with his wife and children in the evening.

On the other hand, Fred's job and personal satisfaction are influenced very little by four items on the list, and those automatically become Cs. They are C-1 through C-4, to be done in order of importance, if time is available after the As and Bs are completed. Fred initiated the follow-up letters to teachers—they are desirable but not necessary. C-2 involves a course description change, but Fred could continue to teach 402 in the same manner even without the change, so it does not get a priority. C-3 and C-4 are letter responses that are high on someone else's list but not on Fred's. To accomplish all of the Cs would take about one and a half hours, and Fred feels that greater personal and professional satisfaction will be derived from spending that time on the Bs.

The B-1s will take about an hour and a half. They are related to a workshop that is to be held in four weeks. Fred wants to avoid the stress and pressures of last minute planning, so he is working now toward the completion of two small tasks—preparation of slides and a handout. Although writing (B-2) is important to Fred and provides him with satisfaction, he would not be devastated by not spending an hour writing on this day. Fred has discovered from past experiences, however, that if he sticks to the As and eliminates the Cs, he is likely to get all of the As and Bs done without the stress of hurrying or worrying about getting everything done.

If you were to ask Fred about the Cs, he would say something like this: "I do one of them each day before I go home, and I have one hour on Friday afternoons to tackle as many as I can. After that I don't worry about any of them until someone brings them to my attention. Then I make them Bs."

Some time management experts believe that the ABC method is too confining and doesn't allow for the expectations and demands of others. Certainly the ABC method is effective only if you take the time, each day or week, to list and rank the tasks and activities in your life. If time pressures are not causing stress in your life, setting priorities may actually create stress for you. Since this is contrary to the holistic approach to stress management, do what seems to work best for you. What nourishes one person may poison another—use what works and is best for *you*. Identify what you need and would like to accomplish in a given time period, and then use your time in ways that will yield you the greatest personal and professional satisfaction.

There are many practical ways to set priorities for life. The references at the end of this chapter provide a variety of ways for establishing and writing down priorities. Try them if you like, adapt them for your individual needs, or develop your own. Whichever method of setting priorities you choose to use, consider these points:

1. Identify your major goals—for yourself and your family as well as for your job.
2. List all actions or tasks that will move you toward your goals.
3. Identify the priority items that will yield the most results in each category (self, work, and family).
4. Within reasonable limits, plan your personal priorities first and schedule the rest of the day around them.
5. If you aren't getting results or moving toward your goals, reassess your goals and priorities and how you are spending your time.
6. Be consistent and stick to *your* priorities.

## OBSTACLES TO EFFECTIVE TIME MANAGEMENT

One way to reduce time conflicts and the stress they create is to be aware of obstacles to effective time management. Five such obstacles—procrastination and worry, perfectionism, fear of failure, avoidance versus confrontation, and overwhelming tasks—and a few strategies for dealing with them are examined here.

### Procrastination

Murphy's Law states: "If anything can go wrong—it will."[9] A corollary to Murphy's Law as it applies to procrastination reads: "When procrastinating, things will always go from bad to worse." It's the old idea of moving from the pan into the fire; that is, the flames will create more stress than the heat. One combination that is sure to create distress (stress gone bad) in the lives of humans is procrastination and worry. One seems to feed the other, and often they lead to immobilization—ineffective or nonuse of time.

Procrastination—the putting off of an event or an activity—is the thief of time.[10] The greater the value of the event or activity, the greater the distress that results from putting it off. It may be overwhelming, distasteful, or difficult, but nonetheless one that needs to be done and isn't getting the attention or time it needs. The price that is paid between when you should have started and when you actually do comes in the form of anxiety and worry. Both anxiety and worry can create an imbalance within the body as well as initiating and maintaining a primary-secondary stress cycle.

What are some ways of dealing with procrastination? Wayne Dyer presents a fairly simple yet comprehensive list of techniques in his book, *Your Erroneous Zones*.[11] They make sense and are easy to implement. Dyer calls these "Some Techniques for Ousting This Postponing Behavior":

1. Make a decision to live five minutes at a time. Instead of thinking of tasks in long-range terms, think about now and try to use up a five-minute period doing what you want, refusing to put off anything that would bring about satisfaction.

2. Sit down and get started on something you've been postponing. Begin a letter or a book. You'll find that much of your putting it off is unnecessary since you'll very likely find the job enjoyable, once you give up the procrastination. Simply beginning will help you to eliminate anxiety about the whole project.

3. Ask yourself, "What is the worst thing that could happen to me if I did what I'm putting off right now?" The answer is usually so insignificant that it may jar you into action. Assess your fear and you'll have no reason to hang on to it.

4. Give yourself a designated time slot (say Wednesday from 10:00 to 10:15 P.M.) which you will devote exclusively to the task you've been putting off. You'll discover that the fifteen minutes of devoted effort are often sufficient to see you over the hump of procrastination.

5. Think of yourself as too significant to live with anxiety about the things you have to do. So, the next time you know you are uncomfortable with postponement anxiety, remember that people who love themselves don't hurt themselves that way.

6. Look carefully at your now. Decide what you are avoiding in your current moments and begin to tackle the fear of living effectively. Procrastination is substituting the now with anxiety about a future event. If the event becomes the now, the anxiety, by definition, must go.

7. Quit smoking . . . now! Begin your diet . . . this moment! Give up booze . . . this second. Put this book down and do one push-up as your beginning exercise project. That's how you tackle problems . . . with action now! Do it! The only thing holding you back is you, and the neurotic choices you've made because you don't believe you're as strong as you really are. How simple . . . just do it!

8. Start using your mind creatively in what were previously boring circumstances. At a meeting, change the dull tempo with a pertinent question, or make your mind go off in exciting ways such as writing a poem, or memorizing twenty-five numbers backwards, just for the sheer drill of memory training. Decide to never be bored again.

9. When someone begins to criticize you, ask this question, "Do you think I need a critic now?" Or when you find yourself being a critic,

ask the person in your company if he wants to hear your criticism, and if so, why? This will help you to move from the critic to the doer column.

10. Look hard at your life. Are you doing what you'd choose to be doing if you knew you had six months to live? If not, you'd better begin doing it because, relatively speaking, that's all you have. Given the eternity of time, thirty years or six months make no difference. Your total lifetime is a mere speck. Delaying anything makes no sense.

11. Be courageous about undertaking an activity that you've been avoiding. One act of courage can eliminate all that fear. Stop telling yourself that you must perform well. Remind yourself that doing it is far more important.

12. Decide not to be tired until the moment before you get into bed. Don't allow yourself to use fatigue or illness as an escape or to put off doing anything. You may find that when you take away the reason for the illness or exhaustion—that is, avoidance of a task—physical problems "magically" disappear.

13. Eliminate the words "hope," "wish" and "maybe" from your vocabulary. They are the tools of putting it off. If you see these words creeping in, substitute new sentences. Change

    • "I hope things will work out" to "I will make it happen."

    • "I wish things were better" to "I am going to do the following things to ensure that I feel better."

    • "Maybe it will be okay" to "I will make it okay."

14. Keep a journal of your own complaining or critical behavior. By writing these actions down, you'll accomplish two things. You'll see how your critical behavior surfaces in your life—the frequency, patterns, events, and people that are related to your being a critic. You'll also stop yourself from criticizing because it will be such a pain to have to write in the journal.

15. If you are putting something off which involves others (a move, a sex problem, a new job), have a conference with all involved and ask their opinions. Be courageous about talking of your own fears, and see if you are delaying for reasons that are only in your head. By enlisting the aid of a confidante to help you with your procrastination, you'll have made it a joint effort. Soon you'll dissipate much of the anxiousness that goes along with procrastination by sharing that as well.

16. Write a contract with your loved ones in which you will deliver the goods you want to but which you may have been postponing. Have each party keep a copy of the contract, and build in penalties for defaulting. Whether it's a ball game, dinner out, vacation, or theater visit, you'll find this strategy helpful and personally rewarding, since you'll be participating in events that you also find enjoyable.

17. If you want the world to change, don't complain about it. Do something. Rather than using up your present moments with all kinds of immobilizing anxiety over what you are putting off, take charge of this nasty erroneous zone and live now! Be a doer, not a wisher, hoper or critic.[12]

The first half of the duo is procrastination. The other half is worry. Worrying exaggerates and distorts reality. It generates the stress response and feeds procrastination. It squanders away time (time that could be better spent doing and living) to think about or visualize something which may or may not become a reality.

What do people have to worry about? Just about everything and anything. Some worry about money and bills; some worry about losing a job or gaining a promotion; some worry about inflation and the state of the economy; some worry about growing old; some worry about health and dying from a heart attack or cancer; and still others worry about the unknown, which means they are constantly worrying, because no one knows what the next minute will bring. There are as many things to worry about as the imagination can create. But no amount of worry will ever change the actual event when, and if, it becomes a reality.

Like procrastination, worry is a time robber. It consumes valuable time and energy that is meant for living and experiencing. Worrying can make you fatigued by the end of the day. Excessive fatigue is a common sign of stress. Worry is also one of the underlying causes for much of the stress gone bad that you experience. Ulcers, high blood pressure, tension headaches, heart attacks, and many of the other stress-related diseases have their roots in worry. Worry indicates that you have given up control over your time to the imagination. If you are a worrier, it is time to regain control.

There are some very definite actions that can be taken to reduce the worry time of your life, increase the productive time, and reduce the amount of stress. They are:

1. Realize that worry is a time robber.
2. Make a worry list. Include everything you find yourself worrying about. Give each item a score, from 0 to 10, to indicate the change

accomplished by worry (actions that may have followed your worrying don't count). If your total number of points is zero, read on.

3. Worry, worry, worry, each and every day, for about five minutes. Decide on a time for a worry session, when all you do is worry about the specifics on your list. At the end of the five minutes, pat yourself on the back for restricting your worrying to just five minutes, and move on to the next point.

4. Take action. Many of the items you are worried about can be dealt with by effective planning. This means defining and redefining long-term goals, especially high-priority goals. It also means identifying specific actions that can be taken to move you toward your goals. Give those actions high priority and build them into your daily, weekly, or monthly schedules. If this kind of planning doesn't seem to be moving you toward the goal, you may need to reassess the goal. Perhaps you need to change that goal or eliminate it. But you do not need to worry about it. Worrying just wastes your time and your life.

5. Try to develop a nonworry philosophy based on the idea that life is for living, not worrying.

6. Learn to use your imagination in positive and beneficial ways. Use the exercises described in Chapter 11. Remember that you control your thoughts, that you can encourage or discourage elicitation of the stress response.

These six steps can help you, but only if you use them. When you use time constructively, you are no longer procrastinating or worrying as much. You are in charge, determining the direction and the experiences of your life, and reducing stress.

## Perfectionism

To approach a task with the intent of doing it perfectly is to attempt the impossible. If you try to accomplish the impossible, you invite dissatisfaction, frustration, and stress. Perfectionism can become such an addicting behavior that a person loses the ability to approach tasks in a rational manner. Perfectionists tend to spend an overabundance of time and energy on a few tasks at the expense of others, and such behavior can cause conflict and stress.

One of the ways the perfectionist creates stress is by spending so much time and energy on one task that sight of long-term goals is lost. When these do not get accomplished, the perfectionist is likely to experience frustration because self-expectations are not fulfilled and the person feels dissatisfaction and anxiety about not doing his or her best. In addition, the perfectionist is likely to have difficulty maintaining a satisfactory balance in the time he or she devotes to self, family, and job. This imbalance can create inner conflict and conflicts in relationships with other people. And so the perfectionist experiences stress.

How can a perfectionist reduce the stress in his or her life? There are some steps that can be taken. Most of them focus on perception of life events and involve examination of goals, priorities, and values. If you are a perfectionist, you should:

1. Develop a "hitter's" attitude—recognize that getting a hit three out of ten times at bat is an excellent average for a baseball player. The batter was involved in ten attempts, ten different experiences, and was successful in three of those experiences. All the time, the person was doing, playing, and experiencing in each opportunity. Similarly, as a perfectionist you can benefit from expanding the spectrum of your involvement, not with the intent of being successful but to try new experiences.

2. After examining your goals and establishing priorities for yourself, family, and vocation, set out to accomplish those goals. Begin to expand your horizons and your undertakings. Take time to rethink, replan, and redo within the time structure you have allotted each item. Once you get started, you begin to accumulate experience in handling your life this way, and you will find that it is easier to manage your time and your tasks. When you focus on long-term goals and on achieving balance in your use of time, you will begin to feel less pressure to achieve perfection. This, in turn, will decrease frustration and stress.

3. View "unfinishedness" as an opportunity, not as a problem. Everything we do in one way or another is unfinished. If we redo, add, and revise, both stress and blood pressure are likely to increase. Once you have given a task an appropriate amount of time and effort, move on to other experiences and other life events. If a project or task comes back to you for improvements, view that as another opportunity to establish new time limits and to upgrade the project. A task becomes a problem and a source of stress only when it begins to consume too much of your time and disturbs the balance you are trying to establish among self, family, and job.

These three approaches can help you change your attitudes about the need to achieve perfection. It is important to be aware that making these changes too quickly can lead to frustration and stress. It has taken years and thousands of life experiences to create the inner voice of perfectionism. Move slowly as you explore new attitudes and new ways to reduce stress.

## Fear of Failure

If an event is perceived as threatening, that can arouse fear that elicits the stress response. If you are afraid you will fail at a task, your self-image is threatened. The perfectionist fears failure, and this can lead to an emotional paralysis that is an avoidance of risk. Willington writes, "Fear of failure causes mediocrity. It blinds us from our true talents. It keeps us from actualizing our abilities. It causes us to give up too soon."[13] When fear of failure leads to inaction, unhappiness, dissatisfaction, frustration, and stress are likely to follow.

Fear of failure becomes an obstacle because we live in a culture that places a high value on success, on product rather than process. We learn early in our lives that we will be judged by a standard of excellence based on performance rather than on effort. In such an environment, a child is likely to experience failure—and diminished self-concept—more often than success. And as such experiences accumulate, the child may come to believe that "If I don't try, I can't fail." It is what Dyer refers to as a "do your best neurosis [which] can keep you from trying new activities and enjoying old ones."[14]

Yet Dyer has also suggested that "failure does not exist. Failure is simply someone else's opinion of how a certain act should have been completed."[15] Hugh Prather has said, "There is no such thing as failure, there is only what happens. If I never try anything, I can never learn anything."[16] In the wellness framework, what seems to be a failure, a frustration, or a disappointment can be a blessing in disguise. Such experiences enhance self-awareness and facilitate self-assessment. If we allow ourselves to learn from "failure," we can increase our options, improve the effectiveness with which we use time, and reduce the paralysis of inaction.

Separate your actions from your self-concept. If an activity doesn't turn out as well as you or others expect, speak about your action, not about "what a failure I am." Assess what happened and use what you learn to help you explore new possibilities and different approaches.

Practice positive affirmation statements (Chapter 12). Remember: An imagined experience can generate stress as readily as a real experience. You are what you think you are, and your self-concept is enhanced by constructive use of visualization and positive statements.

Do activities that are related to the things you fear.[17] Perhaps you are afraid to make a change from a high-paying, high-stress job to a lower-paying but less stressful job. Start looking, ask questions, interview, and seek out others who have made such a change. Listen to their positive statements. Discuss the situation with your family, and try to examine all the possible ramifications. At the same time, realize that you can do it if you want to badly enough. Avoidance never leaves one satisfied or fulfilled.

## Avoidance vs. Confrontation

Procrastination, worry, perfectionism, and fear of failure are all avoidance techniques. Whenever you avoid something, time becomes a factor. You may find that you are not using time effectively or that you are not maintaining a balance in time used for self, family, and vocation. Conflict and stress are likely to result.

## Overwhelming Tasks

How often have you encountered an overwhelming task or situation and wondered where to begin and how to find enough time to complete it? A large block of time is set aside to tackle it. But you remain flexible for interruptions, emergencies, and daily routines, and that large block of time gets smaller and smaller. It may get so small that there isn't enough time to complete the task.

Perfectionism and fear of failure may lead to procrastination, and then all three reinforce your perception of the task as overwhelming. And the longer you delay getting started, the less time you have to complete the task, the more overwhelming it is. This cycle, once started, is sure to produce stress and reduce your ability to cope—with an assignment in school, at work, or at home.

Was priority time built into each day or week to tackle small aspects of the overwhelming task? Was maximum use made of that time? Were small parts of the large project undertaken? These are effective ways to approach an overwhelming task, so that you make the best use of available time and reduce the stressors in your life.

Lakein calls such a system the "swiss cheese"[18] method; Girdano refers to it as a social engineering technique.[19] The idea is to reduce the large task to many smaller tasks. Each of these smaller tasks is viewed as an entity, and when all of them are completed, the large task is completed. One of the best ways to diminish the stress of a large task is to break it into smaller, more manageable, tasks.

Effective time management as a part of stress management will enable you to get started *now* and to keep at it until you have reached your goal. Overwhelming tasks really don't have to be stress producers.

Each of us learns, when we are quite young, that not everything encountered in life is pleasurable. Along the way, we are going to have to handle important chores and situations that are downright unpleasant. When faced with a distasteful job or situation, we can confront it head on and deal with it, we can avoid it, or we can find an intermediate approach. Confrontation may generate the stress response, but avoidance may generate ten times as much stress. Avoidance is usually accompanied by worry. These are likely to initiate a primary-secondary stress cycle, which in turn makes the distasteful more distasteful. As Lakein has stated in his book, *How to Get Control of Your Time and Your Life,* [20] the question is not "Will I do it?" but "When?"

If you have weighed all factors and know that the distasteful does, in fact, need to be done, then the most constructive approach is to get started. Once you start, you are using time effectively, and you are also avoiding needless stress. Starting the distasteful may be easier if you consider these points:

1. The distasteful is done best by you. If you pass your dirty work on to someone else, it may come back to you, demanding more time and generating more stress.
2. A distasteful task rarely goes away when ignored.
3. A distasteful task never gets easier later.
4. The longer you delay doing a distasteful task, the more unpleasant it becomes. [21]

If you confront a distasteful task and dispose of it, you prevent stress from developing, and you are free to go on to other important—and perhaps pleasant—tasks.

## TIME MANAGEMENT AND STRESS REDUCTION

The more effectively you are able to control and direct the time in your life, the more opportunities you have for yourself, your family, and your vocation. Time management enables you to plan and organize time effectively, so that you can control the experiences and opportunities that life affords you and perhaps make life less stressful.

Reducing stress by gaining control of time is both a matter of social engineering and personality engineering, as described by Girdano and Everly in *Controlling Stress and Tension: A Holistic Approach.* [22] You must make a conscious effort to intervene and change those factors that are causing conflict, stimulus overload, stimulus underload, dissatisfaction, frustration and, as a result, stress. To reduce stress, you have to plan your life—your time. Assessment, intervention, nourishment, reinforcement, and motivation—all these will help you to plan your use of time so that you spend time productively and in ways that are fulfilling.

You may find it helpful to think of each day—each twenty-four hours—as three eight-hour periods. There are eight hours for work, eight hours for renewal and relationships, and eight hours for sleeping. This division of time is a natural one that provides balance and can reduce stress, especially if you are both flexible and effective in your use of time.

Remember: The goal is to use time more effectively, to maintain an appropriate pace, and to view stress in appropriate terms. If you are comfortable with how you are using time, you may not want to make changes in your time management—such unnecessary change can, indeed, create stress. But if you assess your life and decide that change is desirable, improved time management can help you to achieve internal balance and harmony.

## SUMMARY

Stress reduction involves a careful examination of your entire life and the use of intervention strategies where appropriate. Time management—how you use it and how effectively you apportion it among the important areas of your life—can reduce elicitation of the stress response. The types of stress that result from conflicts in poor time management include hurry sickness, ineffective pacing, stimulus overload, stimulus underload, anxiety and worry, and negative cycles. When the result of these conflicts is dissatisfaction, frustration, or unhappiness, stress is eminent.

One way to reduce conflicts and stress is to better manage your time. Effective time management encompasses awareness of the sources and results of time conflicts and of ways to intervene to eliminate these conflicts. Effective time management begins when you take the time needed to identify important values, goals, and priorities in your life. Value clarification includes examination of purpose, meaning, joy, and pleasure. Goals are statements that provide the direction. And priorities are subjective rankings (of the tasks, items, and life events) that help you move toward goals.

In striving for effective time management and stress reduction, you may encounter several obstacles, including procrastination and worry, perfectionism, fear of failure, and avoidance. Intervention strategies for dealing with these include (1) awareness of the obstacle, and (2) practicing suggested activities to help deal with the obstacle. These strategies should be implemented in a slow, deliberate, and planned manner, so that you do not generate needless stress.

### Notes

1  David Rood and Richard Detert, "Personal Satisfaction Index" (Paper distributed at the University of Wisconsin-La Crosse, 1980).

2 Meyer Friedman and Ray H. Rosenman, *Type A Behavior and Your Heart* (Greenwich: Fawcett, 1975), p. 87.

3 Hans Selye, *Stress Without Distress* (New York: New American Library, 1974), pp. 74–75.

4 John S. Hoyt, *Personal Time Management and Effective Administration: In Pursuit of the 60-Minute Hour* (Minneapolis: University of Minnesota, Agricultural Extension Service, 1979).

5 Daniel A. Girdano and George S. Everly, *Controlling Stress and Tension: A Holistic Approach* (Englewood Cliffs, N. J.: Prentice-Hall, 1979), p. 133.

6 John J. Pilch, "Spiritual Wellness" (Presentation at the University of Wisconsin-La Crosse, 1979).

7 John J. Pilch, "Spiritual Wellness Reflection Guide" (Paper distributed at the University of Wisconsin-La Crosse, 1979).

8 Edward R. Dayton, *Tools for Time Management: Christian Perspectives on Managing Priorities* (Grand Rapids: Zondervan, 1979), p. 81.

9 Arthur Bloch, *Murphy's Law and Other Reasons Why Things Go Wrong!* (Los Angeles: Price/Stern/Sloan, 1977), p. 11.

10 Jim Davidson, *Effective Time Management: A Practical Workbook* (New York: Human Science Press, 1978), p. 75.

11 Wayne W. Dyer, *Your Erroneous Zones* (New York: Avon, 1977), pp. 194–197.

12 Ibid., p. 98.

13 Ron Willington, "Breaking Out of the Anxiety Box," *Success Unlimited* 27 (1980): 17.

14 Dyer, *Your Erroneous Zones*, p. 134.

15 Ibid., p. 133.

16 Hugh Prather, *I Touch the Earth, the Earth Touches Me* (New York: Doubleday, 1972).

17 Willington, *Breaking Out of the Anxiety Box*, p. 18.

18 Alan Lakein, *How to Get Control of Your Time and Your Life* (New York: Signet, 1974), p. 71.

19 Girdano and Everly, *Controlling Stress and Tension*, p. 137.

20 Hoyt, *Personal Time Management*, pp. 1–2.

21 Lakein, *How to Get Control of Your Time*, p. 127.

22 Girdano and Everly, *Controlling Stress and Tension*.

23 From "The Time of Your Life," film based on Alan Lakein's book *How to Get Control of Your Time and Your Life*, 1974.

## References

Bloch, Arthur. *Murphy's Law and Other Reasons Why Things Go Wrong!* Los Angeles: Price/Stern/Sloan, 1977.

Davidson, Jim. *Effective Time Management: A Practical Workbook.* New York: Human Science Press, 1978.

Dayton, Edward R. *Tools for Time Management: Christian Perspectives on Managing Priorities.* Grand Rapids: Zondervan, 1979.

Dyer, Wayne W. *Your Erroneous Zones.* New York: Avon, 1977.

Ellis, Albert, and Harper, Robert A. *A Guide to Rational Living.* Hollywood, California: Wilshire, 1973.

Friedman, Meyer, and Rosenman, Ray H. *Type A Behavior and Your Heart.* Greenwich: Fawcett, 1975.

Girdano, Daniel A., and Everly, George S. *Controlling Stress and Tension: A Holistic Approach.* Englewood Cliffs, N. J.: Prentice-Hall, 1979.

Glasser, William. *Reality Therapy: A New Approach to Psychiatry.* New York: Harper & Row, 1965.

Hoyt, John S. *Personal Time Management and Effective Administration: In Pursuit of the Sixty-Minute Hour.* University of Minnesota: Agricultural Extension Service, 1979.

Lakein, Alan. *How to Get Control of Your Time and Your Life.* New York: Signet, 1974.

Peele, Stanton, and Brodsky, Archie. *Love and Addiction.* New York: Taplinger, 1975.

Pilch, John J. "Spiritual Wellness." Paper presented at the University of Wisconsin-La Crosse, 1979.

Pilch, John J. "Spiritual Wellness Reflection Guide." Paper distributed at the University of Wisconsin-La Crosse, 1979.

Prather, Hugh. *I Touch the Earth, the Earth Touches Me.* New York: Doubleday, 1972.

Raths, L.; Harmin, M.; and Simon, S. *Values and Teaching.* Columbus: Charles E. Merrill, 1966.

Rood, David, and Detert, Richard A. "Personal Satisfaction Index." Paper distributed at the University of Wisconsin-La Crosse, 1980.

Selye, Hans. *Stress Without Distress.* New York: New American Library, 1974.

"The Time of Your Life." Film based on Alan Lakein's book *How to Get Control of Your Time and Your Life,* 1974.

Tubesing, Donald A. *Stress Kills: A Structured Strategy for Helping People Manage Stress More Effectively.* Oakbrook, Ill.: Whole Persons Associates, 1979.

Willington, Ron. "Breaking Out of the Anxiety Box." *Success Unlimited* 27 (1980): 17–18.

# 15

**▆▆▆▆▆▆▆▆▆**

# NUTRITION AND EXERCISE

A comprehensive stress management program includes many components. From these each individual must select the ones that meet his or her particular needs. Some stress management techniques will be more appropriate for you than others. Almost everyone, though, will want to include attention to nutrition and exercise, both vital factors in achieving and maintaining good health.

## NUTRITION

How are stress and nutrition related? The various systems of the body communicate with one another. What affects one affects the others, and the body reacts as a unit. Some foods can elicit the stress response. Some nutrients are needed in larger quantities when you are under stress, and others are important to the stress response. The stress response alters digestion and absorption processes, and so can lead to ulcers or other digestive problems over a long period of time. And the stress response not only affects various bodily functions, it also depends on other body systems for its effective elicitation.

How does nutrition relate to a stress management program? People who are healthy are not as susceptible to various illnesses as people who are not. Sound nutritional habits contribute to a person's overall health and, thus, provide increased resistance to stress. Remember: The body responds as a whole, with all organ systems contributing to health or illness.

The individual's response to acute or chronic stress has an impact on the relationship between stress and nutrition. When exposed to either chronic or acute stress, many people respond by altering their normal behavior patterns. Alterations may include increasing (or decreasing) work load and physical exertion level as well as changes in sleeping and eating habits. If the altered habits are detrimental to health, the result may be secondary stressors that make the individual even more vulnerable to the primary stressor. Thus, these secondary stressors can contribute to a more prolonged or severe reaction to the primary stressor.

Stress and nutrition are also interrelated in the stress response. Some foods can alter the body's homeostatic equilibrium and produce a response that mimics the stress response. The stress response alters digestion and absorption processes, and these changes can lead directly (or indirectly) to ulcers, a stress-related disease of the digestive system. It has been suggested that when the body is under stress, the need for specific nutrients necessary for good health is altered.

## Chemical Agents

Drugs are ingested regularly by Americans, and many of these drugs trigger the stress response. The most consumed drug in the United States is caffeine, which is contained in various amounts in coffee, cola beverages, tea (except herbal teas), and various forms of chocolate. These foods and beverages are consumed regularly by many people during a normal day. The level of the stress response elicited is determined by the amount of the chemical ingested; by limiting the intake, you can control the extent of the mimicked response elicited.

Another drug that is widely used is nicotine. Although nicotine is not a nutrient, it is mentioned here because so much is ingested by so many people. Nicotine activates the sympathetic nervous systems in much the same way that caffeine does. In addition, smokers, for unknown reasons, have decreased serum vitamin C levels, and vitamin C is important in combating stress, as is described below.[1]

## Nutrients

Elicitation of the stress response can alter the body's use of various nutrients. Girdano and Everly tell us:

Especially during stressful times, high levels of certain vitamins are needed to maintain properly functioning nervous and endocrine systems: These are vitamin C and the vitamins of the B complex, particularly vitamin B-1 (thiamine), B-2 (riboflavin), niacin, B-5 (pantothenic acid), B-6 (pyridoxine hydrochloride), and choline. These B-complex vitamins are important components of the stress response in that deficiencies of vitamins B-1, B-5, and B-6 can lead to anxiety reactions, depression, insomnia, and cardiovascular weaknesses, while vitamins B-2 and niacin deficiencies have been known to cause stomach irritability and muscular weakness. Their depletion lowers your tolerance to, and ability to cope with stressors.[2]

Girdano and Everly also point out that vitamins play a role in the stress response. Vitamins B-1, B-2, and niacin have a role in carbohydrate metabolism and gluconeogenesis, both of which are increased during stress. Vitamins B-5, C, and choline are needed during the production of the adrenal hormones secreted during the elicitation of the stress response.[3]

It is a widely held hypothesis that the need for vitamin C increases when a person is under stress. The stress response causes the release of adrenal hormones (epinephrine and norepinephrine) from the adrenal gland, where a large amount of vitamin C is stored. The production of adrenal hormones to replenish those released during stress is accelerated by vitamin C. Furthermore, thyroid hormone production, which regulates the metabolic rate of the body, requires vitamin C for the synthesis of the thyroid hormone and thyroxine. Because the metabolic rate increases when the body is under stress, so does the body's need for vitamin C.

Vitamin C is also an important agent in the healing of wounds, because it helps maintain resistance to infection. Therefore, any major body stress—such as injury, fracture, shock, or general illness—depletes the body's supply of vitamin C and necessitates increased intake of vitamin C. (Fevers, the stress of injury, and surgery increase the body's need for riboflavin.)[4]

## The Digestion and Absorption Processes

When the adrenal gland (which sits on top of the kidney) is exposed to a stressor, it releases a group of hormones called catecholamines—the adrenal hormones. These are carried throughout the body and elicit the classic stress response and the corresponding physiological changes that enable the person to confront or escape the danger.

In addition, blood is drawn away from the digestive system and the flow of digestive juices (such as bile, gastric, pancreatic, and intestinal juices) is halted. Thus, at a time of extreme danger, digestion and absorption processes are altered. This response is needed during a life-threatening event, to enable the individual to escape or to prepare to fight. However, when modern people are confronted regularly with stressors that are not life threatening, the same response occurs. E. Whitney and M. Hamilton describe the sequence of events, in the digestive system, after exposure to a stressor, and they explain what can result if prolonged or repeated exposure occurs:

> Fear or anxiety can shut off the flow of pancreatic juice to the duodenum and can increase peristalsis so that acid contents of the stomach are dumped into the duodenum at a time when the duodenum is unprepared for the acid. The duodenum does not have a thick mucous coat to protect itself against acid; consequently, it relies on hormones to inform the pancreas that acid contents are on the way and that the pancreas must secrete alkaline fluid into the duodenum to neutralize the acid. If alkaline ions are not present when the chyme mixed with acid arrives, and if this is a frequent occurrence, eventually an erosion of the duodenum mucosa may result; that is, an ulcer may form.[5]

Ulcers are considered to be stress-related and are thought to be caused by the body's reaction to various emotions (such as worry, anxiety, frustration, and rage) over a prolonged period of time. Remember: Worry is a special type of stressor that keeps the stress response elicited even when the primary stressor is gone.

## EXERCISE

Contemporary research on the stress response validates Charles Darwin's theory that the fittest survive. Those who survive are those whose stress response is most refined, and this ever more complex stress response is passed along in the genes from one generation to the next.

The stress response, designed to prepare the individual for the activity of fight or flight, has not had time to adapt to our lesser involvement in physical activity. Nevertheless, the body continues to respond by producing—even if in different amounts and proportions than in the past—substances that must be dissipated. Stress triggers increased levels of adrenalin and other hormones, and those levels need to be reduced, if not by fight or flight then by some other means.

The immediate physical activity of fight or flight is nature's way of returning the body to its normal homeostatic state. Modern people often do not have the "luxury" of immediate physical activity, because the response usually is elicited by events that are not life threatening. Increased work loads, time deadlines, the telephone, rising prices, fuel shortages, and even the news can trigger the stress response. In most situations, physical activity is not necessary, because the event is not life threatening. Often the arousal level is not consciously perceived by the individual; consequently, it is not dealt with in any way.·

Exercise is one means of dealing with the stress response. Physical exercise helps reduce the aroused state by reducing the adrenal hormones in the blood system and, thus, the triggering effect in the various target organs. Ask a person who is under stress and performs some exercise. After strenuous exercise, many report that they feel more self-assured and more relaxed, that a big load has been lifted off their shoulders.

Once the stress response is initiated, exercise often deals with the arousal level more effectively than other means, including relaxation. Relaxation can inhibit arousal and is helpful in reducing an arousal level, but in the latter situation often not as effectively as exercise.

Furthermore, when using the whole-person approach, exercise has another, more indirect effect on the stress response. When a person disciplines him or her self by developing and following a regular exercise program, the level of mental as well as physical health is increased. The person is likely to feel healthier and stronger and to have an increased ability to cope. Simply, exercise makes us feel better about ourselves. Exercise can help prevent the stress response because it decreases our reaction to future stress by increasing our self-esteem. Exercise is a natural form of expression and can bring pleasure, exhilaration, self-assurance, and satisfaction to our lives.

## CONCLUSION

Wellness is a lifelong process; becoming healthier is also a lifelong endeavor. Neither occurs overnight, nor can positive behaviors be forgotten once a desired level occurs. Healthy behavior patterns continually need to be nourished.

Stress management is an important component in a health program. Stress management is not a cure-all, but when coupled with other positive health behaviors, such as physical fitness, nutritional awareness, and emotional stability, stress management can enhance health, happiness, and fulfillment in life.

This page is not the end. On the contrary, you are at the beginning of your stress management program. Today, right now, this very second, is the beginning of the rest of your life, and stress management is a lifelong process. Stress management is a way of life.

## Notes

1 Eleanor Whitney and Eva May Hamilton, *Understanding Nutrition* (St. Paul: West Publishing Company, 1977), p. 316.

2 Daniel A. Girdano and George S. Everly, *Controlling Stress and Tension: A Holistic Approach* (Englewood Cliffs, N. J.: Prentice-Hall, 1979), p. 91.

3 Ibid., pp. 91–92.

4 Corinne H. Robinson, *Fundamentals of Normal Nutrition* (New York: Macmillan, 1978), p. 176.

5 Whitney and Hamilton, *Understanding Nutrition*, p. 194.

## References

Briggs, G. M., and Calloway, D. H. *Nutrition and Physical Fitness.* Philadelphia: W. B. Saunders, 1979.

Girdano, Daniel A., and Everly, George S. *Controlling Stress and Tension: A Holistic Approach.* Englewood Cliffs, N. J.: Prentice-Hall, 1979.

Robinson, Corinne H. *Fundamentals of Normal Nutrition.* New York: Macmillan, 1978.

Vander, Arthur J.; Sherman, James H.; and Luciano, Dorothy S. *Human Physiology and the Mechanism of Body Function.* New York: McGraw-Hill, 1970.

Whitney, Eleanor, and Hamilton, Eva May. *Understanding Nutrition.* St. Paul: West, 1977.

Williams, Sue R. *Nutrition and Diet Therapy.* St. Louis: C. V. Mosby, 1977.

# EPILOGUE

Matajura wanted to become a great swordsman, but his father said he wasn't quick enough and could never learn. So Matajura went to the famous dueller, Banzo, and asked to become his pupil. "How long will it take me to become a master?" he asked. "Suppose I became your servant, was with you every minute; how long?"

"Ten years," said Banzo.

"My father is getting old. Before ten years have passed, I will have to return home to take care of him. Suppose I work twice as hard; how long will it take me?"

"Thirty years," said Banzo.

"How is that?" asked Matajura. "First you say ten years. Then when I offer to work twice as hard, you say it will take three times as long. Let me make myself clear: I will work unceasingly: No hardship will be too much. How long will it take?"

"Seventy years," said Banzo. "A pupil in such a hurry learns slowly."*

*Zen Buddhism. Mount Vernon, N.Y.: The Peter Pauper Press, 1959, p. 36.

# INDEX